INTEGRATE:

The Secret To Harmony
&
The Pursuit of Purpose

ANGEL LOPEZ

ISBN: 979-8-9905529-0-6

DEDICATION

To: Ares, Mars & Freya.

TABLE OF CONTENTS

Chapter 1 **INTEGRATE:** It's A Lifestyle 3

Summary: Feeling overwhelmed juggling life's demands? Discover "integration," a holistic approach to weaving health, growth, wealth, and relationships into a tapestry of well-being. Each pillar supports the others, like a strong foundation fueling meaningful success. Forget the "one-size-fits-all" approach; this book empowers you to craft your unique balance. Feeling lost? Re-evaluate your priorities and take steps towards a life that feels truly yours. Explore stories, inspiring examples, and even mind-shaping secrets on your journey to a life that thrives, not just survives. 3

Chapter 2 **SHADOWS OF OUR PAST:** Why We Make Bad Choices? 13

Summary: It is not our fault. We are a cumulation of our environment, peers, and institutions molding us from childhood. This chapter empowers us to break free. By understanding the hidden forces guiding us, we can gain self-awareness, define our future, and create a supportive environment. Rewrite the script! Practice new behaviors, let go of negative influences, and march forward to progress. Remember, we are not a prisoner of the past. We have the power to create a life that truly reflects our dreams and aspirations. This is just the beginning. Explore a new perspective, seek guidance if needed, and embrace the expedition.
.... 13

Chapter 3 **TAKE THE DRIVER SEAT:** Integrate Your Life 38

Summary: Grab life by the wheel and stop being a watcher from the passenger seat. This chapter encourages self-awareness, proactive goal setting, and consistent action to empower us to create the life we truly desire. We delve into past influences shaping your present choices, then work to design a dream life using specific goals in health, wealth, relationships, and growth with the goal to build unshakeable confidence through bold actions, clear communication, and self-compassion. Each step deposits courage into our "confidence bank," boosting our power and presence. Finally, we learn to embrace our authentic self, flaws and all, to attract the right people and live with purpose. Remember, we are the architect of our journey. Take the wheel and drive the life you deserve 38

Chapter 4 **SELFISH IS GOOD:** What Do You Really Want? 66

Summary: Labels, both praise and criticism, box us in. Stop listening! Discover the real "you" by defying limitations and prioritizing desires. It's okay to be "selfish"; prioritize your well-being, set boundaries, and stop being a pushover. Craft your dream life, not someone else's. You radiate power when you authentically connect with others and inspire their own growth. Take the wheel of your life! Envision your ideal self and commit to the journey. It's time to ditch the labels and unlock your authentic, empowered potential. 66

Chapter 5 **PLAN TO WIN:** One Action Every Moment
.... 78

Summary: Unleash your power by breaking free from programmed patterns and challenge your routines. You're grinding DAY-BY-DAY for your goals; a planner is the way to keep score. Build your action roadmap using tools like daily planners, hyper-focus blocks, and SMART goals. Check off tasks as accomplishments to track progress and prioritize. Become a laser-focused achiever, small actions fueled by intention and repetition lead to big victories! 78

Chapter 6 **REVISIT YOUR LIFE:** Playful Action Fuels Happiness 97

Summary: After going through this journey, you have become a new person. You probably knew that the person that started this planner would not remain the same, but now it is your time to reassess your cause and start again another year. Conscious introspection leads to action, embrace life's challenges with a light heart and detach from worst-case scenarios. Focus on desired outcomes, cultivate a positive outlook, and set healthy boundaries. Don't demand, collaborate! Request things that align with others' best interests for mutual success. Revisit your core values and ensure your daily choices reflect them. Take proactive steps to move closer to your vision. Remember, life is a playground, and a battlefield. Play boldly, act purposefully, and fuel your happiness! 97

Chapter 7 **THE END:** Resources & Readings 103

DISCLAIMER

LIMITS OF LIABILITY & DISCLAIMER OF WARRANTY

INTEGRATE

It's A Lifestyle

"Man becomes whole, integrated, calm, fertile, and happy when (and only when) the process of individuation is complete, when the conscious and the unconscious have learned to live at peace and to complement one another." [1]

- Carl Jung

Summary: Feeling overwhelmed juggling life's demands? Discover "integration," a holistic approach to weaving health, growth, wealth, and relationships into a tapestry of well-being. Each pillar supports the others, like a strong foundation fueling meaningful success. Forget the "one-size-fits-all" approach; this book empowers you to craft your unique balance. Feeling lost? Re-evaluate your priorities and take steps towards a life that feels truly yours. Explore stories, inspiring examples, and even mind-shaping secrets on your journey to a life that thrives, not just survives.

---

[1] Freeman, John, ed. 1968. "Introduction." In Man and His Symbols. Dell Publishing. p. viii

Drowning in Life? Integrate

Are you juggling work, family, and personal goals, feeling like you're constantly treading water? You're not alone. This book is for the countless individuals, exhausted yet driven, trying to hold it together while moving forward, striving for success and fulfillment. Are you a busy professional striving for career success, but want to do it without sacrificing family time? An entrepreneur juggling the burning desire to build a dream, but battling to stay healthy and grounded? Or simply someone yearning to live a life of purpose and meaning? If you answered yes to any of these, then "INTEGRATE" is for you. This book aims to help you find fulfillment by integrating key areas of life: health, personal growth, wealth, and relationships.

Integrate[2] **(verb)** in·te·grate | \ ˈin-tə-ˌgrāt \
integrated; integrating
Definition of *integrate transitive verb*
1: to form, coordinate, or blend into a functioning or unified whole : UNITE
2a: to incorporate into a larger unit. **b:** to unite with something else
3a: *integrate* school districts. **b:** to end the segregation of and bring into equal membership in society or an organization
4: to find the integral of (something, such as a function or equation)

I'm sure we have all set goals that when we accomplished them, we realized: "I have the promotion I always wanted but I have to work a lot more now and can't spend the evening with my family," or "I'm finally married, but my woman is lazy and doesn't even want wash the dishes." Whether we were friends before you picked up

---

[2] "Integrate." Merriam-Webster.com Dictionary, Merriam-Webster, https://www.merriam-webster.com/dictionary/integrate.

this book or are just connecting now, know this: I've been there, and together, we can find a better way. This book is a guide to: identify personal values and goals, uncover areas of imbalance, develop practical tools and strategies for each area, design an action plan to achieve an integrated life, and various other tools and techniques to support the goal.

A Symphony of Being

The secret lies in integration, finding synergy in as many areas of our lives to reduce how much we have to split ourselves. This means that our work, our relationships, our health, and our personal growth are all aligned with our values and goals. If we win, our spouse, or boss wins. If they help us win, they win more. Imagine life not as a chaotic juggling act, but as a beautiful tapestry woven from four essential threads: health, personal growth, wealth, and relationships. Each thread strengthens the others, creating a magnificent tapestry of purpose and well-being. Living an integrated life means feeling a sense of purpose and fulfillment, making a positive impact on the world around us, and feeling good about ourselves. The best part is that it is never too late to integrate these principles and create a life that feels good inside and out.

Take a deep breath and ask yourself, what truly matters to me? What does "success" look like on my terms? Could it be feeling energized for work because you prioritize healthy habits? Making better financial decisions with the wisdom gained from personal growth? There's no one-size-fits-all approach. It's about creating harmony between these areas based on our values and goals. Do you want to be a fit couple who works remotely, or runs a business together, and can travel with the whole family whenever you want? One example of what an Integrated Life means is Grant

Cardone.[3] He runs multiple business that could demand of him to be in three different states the same day, yet is able to spend time with family and friends and keep up with his health. How? He included his wife and kids in his business so he travels with them and they support him, and he bought a wellness company synergistic to his current businesses to supplement his exercise routine.

Maybe you want to keep employees happier, resulting in higher productivity and retention? Of course, there's the massive Silicon Valley tech campuses that provide every amenity making it more desirable to be at work than going home. In a microscale, I've visited companies with perks like gyms, car wash services, babysitting, and cafeterias that sell a full dinner to-go to skip the cooking. Others provide social areas with ping pong tables and fully stocked bars for happy hour. Yet, the most impressive to date; a dog park with the option to bring your pets anytime. Employees finish the workday with their workout done, dinner ready, and pick up their kid at the front desk on their way out. These companies integrate many of the impediments that make it hard to maintain a work-life balance. Of course, there is no one right way to live an integrated life. What matters is to find what works for us resulting in the maximum amount of fulfilment, achievement, and completeness that came from our choices. Feeling lost or unfulfilled may be the best time to take a step back and reevaluate our priorities. Time to ask ourselves what is important and what we want to achieve in our lifetime. Once we have a better understanding of what we want, we can make changes that will help us live a more integrated life.

---

[3] "The Official Website of Grant Cardone." Grant Cardone - 10X Your Business and Life, 14 June 2018, grantcardone.com/.

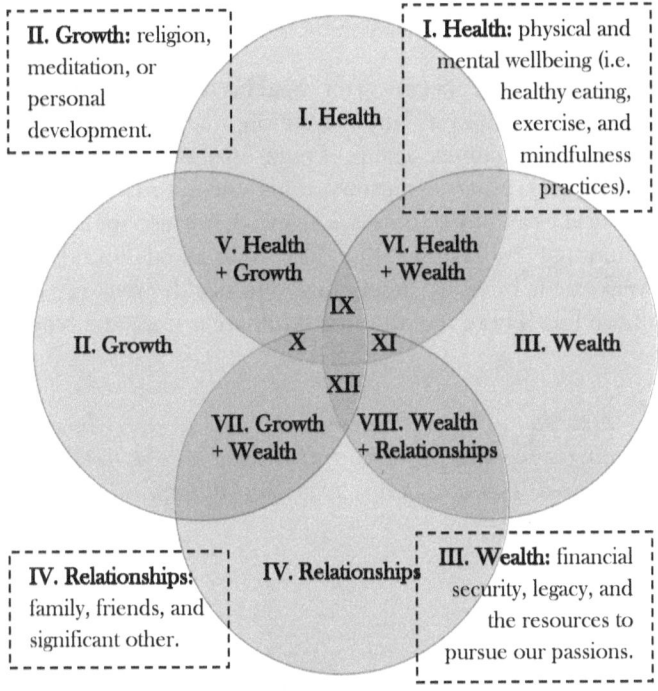

What an integrated life might look like:

❖ Passionate about our work, and using our skills to make a difference in the world.

❖ Strong relationships, feeling supported and loved by family and friends.

❖ Taking care of our physical and mental health to feel healthy and energized.

❖ Always be learning and growing to feel challenged and stimulated.

The Four Pillars of Integration, The Hierchy of Fulfillment

The first pillar begins with **health**, the foundation of everything. Before any ambition, any dream, and relationship; comes health. Think of it as the fertile soil where everything else grows. This encompasses not just physical health (diet, fitness, longevity), but also mental and emotional well-being. Just like a cracked foundation weakens a building, neglecting our health weakens our entire life. There are no more other areas if we are dead.

Health: *The foundation of everything, encompassing physical and mental wellbeing (i.e. healthy eating, energy, exercise, and mindfulness practices).*

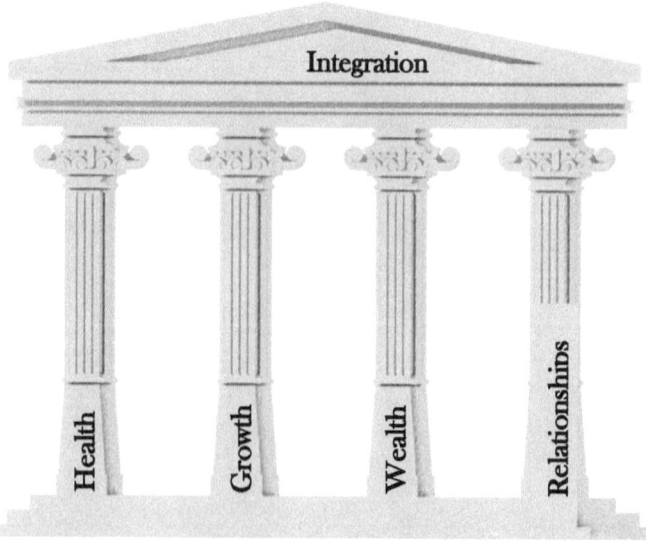

Next is **growth**. This isn't just about acquiring knowledge, but about nurturing wisdom. Whether our inspiration comes from religion, meditation, personal development, or life experiences; growth fuels our journey. Remember, winning the lottery without wisdom is like living in a sandcastle. The tide washes it all away. The learnings in finance and investment is what will let us keep it and grow it.

> **Growth:** *Seeking wisdom through religion, meditation, or personal development. The journey of continuous learning and self-improvement.*

The third area in the hierarchy is **wealth**. Once we've built a strong foundation and cultivated wisdom, it's time to build wealth. But remember, wealth is a tool, not an end-goal. It's the ability to support our lifestyle, fuel our passions, and leave a legacy. Without the right perspective, wealth becomes a heavy burden, not a springboard to freedom. Ultimately as humans we are born, we acquire resources, reproduce and die.

> **Wealth:** *Not just about money, but financial security and the resources to pursue our passions. This includes financial literacy to leave a legacy, smart investments, and conscious spending.*

Finally, we reach the heart of it all, **relationships**. The flame that ignites it all. Family, friends, loved ones; the fire that fuels our journey. Imagine working our whole life, finally achieving the ultimate success; only to realize we have no one to share it with as we sit in the dark. Have you noticed once we meet our ideal partner, we are happy and everything feels worthwhile? Fulfillment comes from strong connections that bring joy and meaning to life.

> **Relationships:** *The connections that bring joy, support, and love into our life. Whether it's family, friends, or a significant other, nurturing these bonds is essential.*

Exercise: Integrate

Envision how the ideal scenario would look for each key area. What if I had achieved the outcome (i.e. *[Health + Growth]: I am 220lbs at 12% bodyfat + I meditate for 15 minutes daily for mental clarity)*?

V. [Health + Growth]:

VI. [Health + Wealth]:

VII. [Growth + Wealth]:

VIII. [Wealth + Relationships]:

Exercise: Integrate (continue)

Now envision how the ideal scenario would look when combining each key area further.

IX.[Health + Growth]] + [Health + Wealth]:

X. [Health + Growth] + [Growth + Wealth]:

XI. [Health + Wealth] + [Wealth + Relationships]:

XII. [Growth + Wealth] + [Wealth + Relationships]:

Summary:

Remember, it is never too late to start living an integrated life. No matter where we are in our life, we can make changes that will help us feel more fulfilled and purposeful. Don't be afraid to take the first step. The journey to an integrated life is a journey worth taking.

1) Take holistic approach to weaving health, growth, wealth, and relationships into a tapestry of well-being.

2) Each pillar supports the others, like a strong foundation fueling meaningful success.

3) Forget the "one-size-fits-all" approach; this book empowers you to craft your unique balance.

4) Re-evaluate your priorities and take steps towards a life that feels truly yours.

SHADOWS OF OUR PAST

Why We Make Bad Choices?

"I am not what we happened to me, but what I choose to become...Actual: It is not I who create myself, rather I happen to myself." [4]

- Carl Jung

Summary: It is not our fault. We are a cumulation of our environment, peers, and institutions molding us from childhood. This chapter empowers us to break free. By understanding the hidden forces guiding us, we can gain self-awareness, define our future, and create a supportive environment. Rewrite the script! Practice new behaviors, let go of negative influences, and march forward to progress. Remember, we are not a prisoner of the past. We have the power to create a life that truly reflects our dreams and aspirations. This is just the beginning. Explore a new perspective, seek guidance if needed, and embrace the expedition.

---

[4] Jung, C. G., et al. The Collected Works of C.G. Jung. Princeton University Press, 1979.

The Echoes of Childhood

Past actions do not always define us, but they sure leave a messy trail of clues about who we are. Like an invisible hand, our past paints our perspective; forming our reactions, habits, biases, and perception of the world. Ultimately this is what creates our experience now. Imagine childhood as the training ground that will imprint us for the rest of our life. Think of a time when a parent or childhood friend has reverted us to behaviors, or thought patterns of the person we were when we were around them in the past. Even if we consciously disagree with something, it can still trigger automatic responses without us realizing it, like echoes from our childhood. Think about when we catch a whiff of our favorite food, we might start salivating; or it could rip us out of the moment and take us to when we were ten waking up on Christmas morning and the smell of moms cooking hits our nose as we are running down the stairs to open presents. That smell is part of the deep neural network of connections and triggers established over our entire life. That means we usually repeat the same actions.

Have you ever wondered why we keep repeating the same patterns despite being aware of the harm and wanting to change? Of course, there are instances where we cannot instantly fix something overnight; like moving away from a bad neighborhood due to financial constraint, or leaving a bad job but having to support a family. It starts with awareness and having a plan. Let's consider our morning routine, do we reach for the same coffee, check the same newsfeed, and eat the same thing? There is a good chance we eat that often. Is it because it is easy? Nutritious? When did we start eating it? Did we do it once and liked the outcome so we continued to do it? This action was introduced, repeated, and reinforced to become a habit. Humans are creatures of habit; we crave the familiar and safe even if it's not serving us. This is why we stay in toxic relationships, why we stay in unfulfilling abusive jobs, and why eat a whole cake right before bed instead of a clean protein. Each time we do something, it strengthens the neural pathways associated with it, making it feel more and more natural. Alcoholics did not wake up one day and decide they were going to develop a dependency to drink. Our past actions and habits define who we were in the past, and our future actions and habits will define who we become. If this if true, what about all our other actions and ideas? An idea would work the same way, it starts as a repeating thought and can become a belief.

The Invisible Hand & Allure of the Familiar

Whether we want to believe we are "individuals" or "unique," most sane people act within a socially self-regulating boundary and with preprogrammed responses. To experience this, visit another country far enough away to be a shock. I first encountered this when I traveled to China. First thing I noticed things are different, but completely normal to everyone there. As I familiarized myself with the culture, values, and way of living; I received a deep insight on the way of life there being much different than ours in America, but at the same time the same.

We have different languages and lifestyles making it seem like another world, but the people all act like one another following the norms of the person next to them, everyone is motivated by self-preservation, both cultures create family units, have traditional foods, etc. The moral is that patterns are usually established by previous generations and if they worked, why fix them. "Culture" has been taught or programed generation over generation. We do what we do because we were programed, and the training was reinforced daily. Every experience and interaction leaves a groove like a vinyl record that continues to replay until we chose to rewrite it. The lessons our parents taught us, our interactions with relatives, a bad review from a teacher; all these instances plant the seeds that blossom into our perspective of the world and ourselves. Comparatively, this is the same process a new hire goes through at job. They are in a sense an infant learning how the business operates, and as they move up the ladder, they pass this company culture to all the new hires. Ultimately, this unchallenged path becomes the invisible strings that bind our thoughts, emotions, and choices to follow the path set before us.

Break The External Influence Mold

Think of interactions with different groups and institutions: co-workers, family, friends; does it feel like we need to wear a "mask" to belong, and cater to the group? Maybe adapt our behavior to fit in? Just like a cult or an abusive relationship, these groups or institutions demand a code of conduct expecting us to give up our personal beliefs, finances, and/or safety in order to operate in, and be accepted by, the group. There is a standard way of acting for every career path, for a date, with family, with friends, etc. If someone is a lawyer, they are going to tend to act like a lawyer, especially around co-workers or at work. An engineer will most likely act, talk, and think like an engineer. A criminal will most likely hang out with other criminals and act and think the same as them.

When these patterns start becoming apparent, it might feel like we have been putting ourselves in a box letting people walk over us to not challenge or offend the group hierarchy. Some of our relationships might start to feel fake, like we are just checking off pre-set social boxes to be able to have one; yet they are only there to see what they can get out of us. In contrast, why do we feel more comfortable in a group with common upbrings? Like "we can be ourselves" and have instant rapport? We have been programed since childhood to believe and act in ways that are socially acceptable, these groups just happened to have been raised in similar environments, income levels, regions, and cultures. Therefore, we have to change less.

Treading a New Trail

Aristotle said, "Give me a child until he is 7 and I will show you the man." [5] This was also stated by St Ignatius Loyola and the Jesuits as, "Give me a child until he is seven and I will show you the man" [6] According to the CDC, the first 8 years can build a foundation for future learning, health and life success.[7] By second grade, us and our kids are fully indoctrinated in a school system created by Rockefeller to create employees.

> *"I don't want a nation of thinkers. I want a nation of workers."* [8]

> \- John D. Rockefeller

We accepted everything they told us at home about religion and politics. Our friends influenced us at school, along with what we saw on TV. Education and Religion are only some of the many institutions that shape our lives

---

[5] Aristotle, The Philosophy of Aristotle

[6] St. Ignacious Loyola and the Jesiut Order

[7] Centers for Disease Control and Prevention. "Early Brain Development and Health." Centers for Disease Control and Prevention, 24 Feb. 2023, www.cdc.gov/ncbddd/childdevelopment/early-brain-development.html.

[8] Attributed to John D. Rockefeller by Jim Marrs in the William Lewis film One Nation Under Siege (2008).

growing up. There are parents, friends, family, television, social media. If our parents are Republican or Democrat, Jewish or Christian, college-educated or blue-collar workers; they are going to instill that "groupthink" or set of values onto us. Most likely our family, parents' friends, the friends we meet, and our communities are going to have similar mindsets. Later, we are probably going to be inclined to live in a community of other people like us, those who we are around become friends, we end up dating in similar groups resulting in children under the same environment to repeat the cycle. Good or bad. The goal is to identify the patterns that hold us back, trace their roots to understand them, and overcome them.

The Puppeteer That Pulls the Strings

This chapter is going to feel like a come down from a hangover of life pinning you to a chair with your eyes forced wide open replaying your blooper reels. When the shocking realization that every decision in our adult life stemmed from the programing of our upbringing, it becomes apparent that we also try "fix everything" with our old patterns. Einstein once allegedly said,

> "*The world that we have made, as a result of the level of thinking we have done thus far, creates problems that we cannot solve at the same level we created them.*"[9]

- Albert Einstein

---

[9] Attributed to Albert Einstein but not confirmed.

It is tempting to blame everything on our past as a convenient excuse for our bad behavior. However, this is also a liberation, our past that made us doesn't define us. We can integrate our faults, negatives, and positives to create a fully congruent ideal integrated self. I first read about this in Meeting the Shadow,[10] a compilation of works delving into the dark side of the human psyche. Basically, tells us forgive ourselves since it is not ALL our fault and accept the duality of nature that we can be bad too, and it is ok...what a relief that we can blame our parents, the school system and the government for our less-than-desirable behavior. But being aware of this, we must also accept that we are in charge and fully responsible for what happens to us next. We were a victim with pre-programed reactions learned from our environment and triggered by feelings. We assigned a meaning to each feeling in our bodies that shapes our perspective, and creates the lens which we see each situation, how we save our experiences into our memory, and how we adapt our personality based on what we thought we experienced; to shape our future choices.

Rewrite the Script

We have been prepared and programmed from childhood to make the choices we are making now. Schools provided us with the education to succeed, churches instilled morality, and family taught us culture and values. Along with this, we all had our peers to impress. With all this training, they sent us off to a world of uncertainty and chaos hoping we make good choices. We met the world with an unshakeable confidence and the world shook it. The ideas

---

[10] Abrams, Jeremiah, and Connie Zweig. Meeting the Shadow: The Hidden Power of the Dark Side of Human Nature. Los Angeles, J.P. Tarcher ; New York, 1991.

we had created are now challenged by the pressures to fit a mold of what we observe in the world, and the confidence we once had is challenged by the skills we need to learn to achieve what we actually want. Life was not the happy fairytale we were promised.

Growing up we were told to go to school, go to college, get a job[11], buy a home[12], and start a family. We do all this, then social media said we needed a mansion, trips on jets, and gold exotic cars; now we are not happy again. We do all this, and now we can't stand the person next to us, get a divorce and lose half our life's work.[13] We went through the motions mindlessly because we were told to do it. Look at one mundane thing we do daily and ask, "why do I continue to do this the same way?" Because we saw it, someone taught us? Is it because we tried it another way and got external pressure to conform?

This applies to everything; is college necessary to be successful, or can I start a business and make 10x more? Do I have to get married; can't I just live with two partners who love me? Do I really have to go to a traditional job, why can't I work from home or learn a skill to make money off that? Fortunately, no matter how deep in the hole or how high in the tower we are, we can always start to take control of our mind, our choices, and ultimately the life we are living. Different people do different things when they hit that point where it is no longer bearable to continue to be running on autopilot. Some get a sports car and leave

---

[11] Rosenthal, Caitlin C. "How Slavery Inspired Modern Business Management." Boston Review, www.bostonreview.net/articles/caitlin-c-rosenthal-accounting-slavery-excerpt/.

[12] "Millennials Are Replaying Their Parents' Housing Market Journey as First-Time Buyers in Their 30s Flood into an Unaffordable Market." Fortune, fortune.com.

[13] Shamsian, Jacob. "A 1947 Ad Campaign Convinced Us All That We Need Diamonds to Get Engaged, and We Still Believe It." Business Insider, www.businessinsider.com/why-do-we-propose-with-diamond-rings.

their family, thinking, "they're weighting me down; I need to go alone to go fast." Others go join a religious cult, "all this freewill is making me sin." This is the moment we realize that what were taught no longer makes sense and we might do something extreme to try to regain control of our life. Ultimately, once the urge to take back control is satisfied, we might be left with some good lessons and no more control than we had initially.

We Acted From Our Past, Charting A New Course

Many of our mental-emotional issues, worries, triggers, interactions, stress management, and relationships are a mix of nature vs nurture. Daniel Goleman writes that we are a combination of nature and nurture. We get a set genetic makeup that reacts with our environment (nature), at the same time, the environment is what shapes it (nurture).

> *"It's not just which genes we were born with, but their expression, that matters....Such insights put to rest the century-old debate on nature versus nurture: do our genes or our experiences determine who we become? That debate turns out to be pointless, based on the fallacy that our genes and our environment are independent of each other; it's like arguing over which contributes more to the area of a rectangle, the length or the width."* [14]

- Daniel Goleman

---

[14] Goleman, Daniel. Social Intelligence: The New Science of Human Relationships. London, Arrow, 2007, p. 150.

We are born like a customized computer. Some computers can have more RAM/Hard Drive space (memory/brain capacity), some have more space for upgrades (size/physicality). That's what we start with. Then we install programs and put the system to use. That determines how it will ultimately operate. Is it a gaming computer? Is it used to compute complex equations? Or is someone writing the next great American novel on it?

Let's take someone who produces more of the stress hormone than the average person as part of their hardware. Cortisol is the bodies alarm system pushing us into action when the time calls. After the danger ends, the levels and the bodies processes, like heart rate, should return to normal function. Yet, if we are constantly stressed, the same cortisol can lead to anxiety, depression, heart disease, memory issues, and weight gain; just to name a few symptoms.[15] This individual is now trying to grow up and create an identity within the social expectations, but they are operation with elevated cortisol. Every interaction, activity, decision is going to be generated from a place of higher stress. Talking to a girl, asking for a raise, or standing up to a partner could have an extra layer of difficulty that needs to be overcome each time. They may be more neurotic than the average person, but depending on the environment, may either develop to be introverted if they are left alone and neglected, or extroverted if they if are taught to cope and develop social skills from an early age. A study examined associations between personality traits and cortisol activity in adolescents. The study stated that:

Neuroticism (N) and introversion (I) were significantly and differentially associated with features of diurnal cortisol patterns. Specifically, a

---

[15] Cassoobhoy, Arefa. "What Is Cortisol?" WebMD, WebMD, 6 Feb. 2017, www.webmd.com/a-to-z-guides/what-is-cortisol.

significant N by gender interaction was observed, demonstrating flatter cortisol rhythms across the waking day among male participants with higher N. Elevated I, however, was associated with lower cortisol awakening responses for both male and female participants, and higher cortisol at the time of waking for male participants only.[16]

The study supports that personality is a significant predictor of cortisol patterns in late adolescence. It was concluded that higher introversion among males was associated with increased cortisol levels and holds a risk factor for social phobia and depression. Higher neuroticism was also associated with a "flatter cortisol slope," or acute stress, among male adolescents. This trend is also associated with shyness in young boys and negative emotions, such as aggression and sadness. Neuroticism has been shown to predict the development of emotional disorders, including major depression, posttraumatic stress disorder (PTSD), phobias, and panic attacks later in life. The data suggests that *trait-like patterns of genetic origin* for higher stress may emerge over time from a history of negative social experiences.

Who we are now, our habits, our mannerisms, and everything else that's part of our character, is a culmination of our: Parents, Friends, Family, Social institutions, Media, and anything else we picked up from our experience in that environment. From the day we are born, we begin to be imprinted by the world around us. Our parents were one of the first influences in most cases. They later introduced

---

[16] Hauner, Katherina K.Y., et al. "Neuroticism and Introversion Are Associated with Salivary Cortisol Patterns in Adolescents." Psychoneuroendocrinology, vol. 33, no. 10, Nov. 2008, pp. 1344–1356, https://doi.org/10.1016/j. *"a flattening of the diurnal cortisol slope can result, in part, from the experience of acute stress"*

us to family where we pick up their habits, and cultural beliefs. They took us to school where we were indoctrinated to our countries school system, and where we picked up other habits to fit in and make friends. As we grew, religion and politics installed their programing too. With all these external influences pressuring us, here comes social media to cement this mess and create a feeling of perpetual inadequacy compensating to fill a mold.

The Power of Repetition, for Bad or for Good

Our behavior and habits come from repetition during our upbringing. Becoming a champion like Mike Tyson, one of the greatest heavyweight boxers of all time, does not come overnight and probably not from an easy life. Tyson's parent died at an early age and he was forced to survive in the high crime neighborhoods of New York. In the streets, he was forced to fight those who ridiculed his voice and lisp, it is noted that his first fight was with a bigger kid who pulled the head off one of his pigeons. By the age of 13, he had been arrested 38 times. When he was a junior in high school he dropped out, at 16 his mother died, and by 18 he made his professional debut to pave his path to become one of the most iconic athletes.[17] Like Napoleon Hill states in Outwitting the Devil:

> *"Nature will not tolerate idleness or vacuums of any sort. All space must be and is filled with something... When the individual does not use the brain for the expression of positive, creative thoughts, nature fills the vacuum by forcing the brain to act upon negative thoughts."..."The person who moves with*

---

[17] Mcneil, William. The Rise of Mike Tyson, Heavyweight. Jefferson, Nc, Mcfarland, 2014.

definiteness recognizes the difference between temporary defeat and failure. When plans fail he substitutes others but he does not change his purpose. He perseveres." [18]

- Napoleon Hill

Habits can also ruin our lives. On the opposite end of the spectrum, look at the countless lottery winners that have lost everything in a few years due to improper management and bad habits. Failure and success does not happen overnight, it is by repetition of habits, a marathon not a sprint. By being aware of our habits now, we can reshape them and develop new ways to interact, or communicate, with our environment and ourselves. If we associate heavily with our past, we might have more trouble making positive change in the future. It all starts with understanding that anything we are now, we can replace with desired traits to make us successful at what we do or want to achieve. It also helps to know that through brain plasticity, our brain is so adaptive that with enough repetition, we can learn virtually any trait; or even learn to walk again after a stroke; as detailed in "The brain that changes itself." [19]

Whether these desired traits include connecting better with those around us, leading groups, or maximizing our performance; they can be learned through actionable repetition. Of course, this is not limited to work because this new mindset, understanding, and techniques will spill-over to the rest of our life and life areas. Virtually any negative trait could be replaced by a more positive one (i.e.

---

[18] Hill, Napoleon. Outwitting the Devil: The Secret to Freedom and Success. New York, Sterling, 2018.
[19] Doidge, Norman. The Brain That Changes Itself: Stories of Personal Triumph from the Frontiers of Brain Science. Melbourne, Scribe, 2007.

listening to understand a spouse, motivating employees, learning a new skill, etc.). All our actions are varying degrees of extremes either moving us closer to, or further from the desired outcome. Fortunately, we can replace where we are now with the desired traits by slowly tipping the scale in the desired direction. Like hot versus cold is temperature and perspective, and love and hate are a way to experience a relationship with another person; the same applies to success and failure, or being a beginner or a professional. Embodying these new desired traits comes from trial and error and constant improvement to refine our way of being. Books like Atomic Habits[20] and The Slight Edge[21] emphasize the power that small habits play in the big picture of attainment of our goals.

Adaptation, The Ultimate Edge

> *"As many more individuals of each species are born than can possibly survive; and as, consequently, there is a frequently recurring struggle for existence, it follows that any being, if it vary however slightly in any manner profitable to itself, under the complex and sometimes varying conditions of life, will have a better chance of surviving, and thus be naturally selected. From the strong principle of inheritance, any selected variety will tend to propagate its new and modified form."* [22]

- Charles Darwin

---

[20] Clear, James. Atomic Habits. New York, Penguin Publishing Group, 16 Oct..

[21] Olson, Jeff, and John David Mann. The Slight Edge. Plano, Texas, Success.

[22] Darwin, Charles. "On the Origin of Species, 1st Edition by Charles Darwin."

Although we can't yet change our physical traits, we can change our mindset and habits. Things seldom go right at the most critical moments; therefore, it is up to us to take control of things we can control. The more experiences we go through, the more we learn and the more we overcome hardship; we become more adept at adapting. We build a resilience to accomplish any task we start. This skill, combined with the foresight to create an end-goal, and working backwards from where we currently stand, shows us the right actions to allow cause and effect do the work.

The more we take action resulting in wins, the more that action gets reinforced; whether it is the best action or not. The more we take action consciously, the more we guide what gets reinforced. The "consciously" part comes from understanding where we are and having a clear sight on where we want to be. Take whatever age we are and assume we are going to live to roughly 80. Although, there is even research showing that making it until 100+ years is not too far from the standard in the near future.[23] Being able to analyze where we want to be in life should take into consideration how we want to be buried, the memories and legacies we want to leave behind, *Memento Mori*.

This mindset also applies to business; we need a plan. We need to know where our competition lies, or where our role model is at. If we are not growing towards surpassing them or reaching that goal, the first question should be: "why do I keep repeating the same actions." Awareness of where we are compared to the worse and the best competitors gives us an understanding on where we fall. To start thinking bigger, look at those who are at the highest levels and think of what they are doing that I am

---

[23] "Jeff Bezos Is Paying for a Way to Make Humans Immortal." Popular Mechanics, 26 Jan. 2022, www.popularmechanics.com/ technology/ startups/a38867242/ jeff-bezos-altos-labs/.

not? What can I can provide that they can't to disrupt them?[24] All this starts with awareness of where we are. It is understanding how to bridge the gap from where we are now, to where we desire to be. With this we can create a roadmap to get there and self-correct along the way. As we are taking these daily actions, our brain develops new neuropathways and we begin to notice that it becomes habit, that is easier and easier to do. One item of caution is Desire.

> *"The will, to become powerful, must be free. If we desire an object, we do not necessarily attract that object, but the object attracts us...The Will accomplishes everything which it does not desire...Those who crave for fame or riches or love are frequently disappointed; the rich miser is poorer than the beggar in the street, and happiness is a shadow that flies before him who seeks it in material pleasures. The surest way to become rich is by being contented with what we have ,- the safest way to obtain power is to sacrifice ourselves for others; and if we desire love, we must distribute the love we possess to others, and then the love of others will descend upon us like the rain descends upon the earth."[25]*

> - *Franz Hartmann*

---

[24] Samit, Jay. Disrupt You!: Master Personal Transformation, Seize Opportunity, and Thrive in the Era of Endless Innovation. New York, Flatiron Books, 2015.

[25] Hartmann, Franz. Magic, White and Black. 1890, p. 260.

If we are chasing something from the wrong mindset, we end up failing, it will consume us; or worse, accomplishing it and feeling worse than we started. Therefore, we should create your roadmap from a place of achievement and not from starvation. The purpose of Integrate is to find the highest level of fulfilment in each area of our life and find a way to weave them into a harmonious existence. This chapter is a starting point, but our journey is unique. Sometimes we might need to seek professional guidance to navigate through some of the more complex relationships or challenges, and that is just fine. It is time to forgive ourselves for past choices, and celebrate the courage it takes to create a new future. Remember, we are not a prisoner of the past, but the author of our story. By understanding the subtle influences shaping our choices, we can rewrite the narrative and create a life that reflects our desires.

Exercise: The Right Reason, What Can We Change?

Is there anything you are perusing for a reason other than the betterment of your situation. In other words, are you chasing something (desire) that will fulfil you, and not for the mere materialistic public opinion? What are some things to start changing now to be our best?

Exercise: The Right Reason, What Can We Change? (continue)

Health:

Personal Growth:

Wealth:

Relationships:

Design Our Simulation, Make New Choices

As long as our fantasies and dreams or "Internal World" (Desired Reality) continues to be different than our reality or "External World" (Current Situation), we will continue to be unexplainedly miserable or at least unfulfilled. Whatever train of thought we follow; whether we believe that if we dream something it is coming from a higher place, or if simply we want something because we saw someone else enjoying it, the situation remains the same...we don't have it. If we see a successful CEO or rapper on TV and we wish we were in their position, we have to ask ourselves, do I really deserve it? Have I done my great work to live the life I want?

We can live a hyper-positive unrealistic life believing that everything is going to go our way if we merely think it hard enough, or we can prepare for war and know that the people that "made it" did it by giving everything of themselves to achieve to these new heights. To get to a new level, we must leave where we are. If we want millions, we have to give up the equivalent to take its' place. Do you have a million things to give up to let a million dollars come in? Most cases we don't. We need to let go of who we are now, we can't live in a mansion with a Ferrari unless we leave the house we live in now. We need to be ready to get rid of everything we are to move into that new house and car. Equally, we need to expand in material wealth, the number of people we help, our influence, and status to even get a million dollars to look our way, let alone be attracted to us. This principle applies to relationships, we need to be the person we want to attract, or have money to bribe them to stay.

External Vs Internal World

"Man lives in two worlds, in his interior and in the exterior world. Each of these worlds exists under conditions peculiar to itself, and that world in which he lives is for the time being the most real to him. When he fully enters his interior world during deep sleep or in moments of perfect abstraction, the forms perceived in the exterior world fade away; but when he awakes into the exterior world the forms seen in his interior state are forgotten, or leave only their uncertain shadows on the sky. To live simultaneously in both worlds is only possible to him who succeeds in harmoniously blending his internal and external worlds into one.

The so-called Real seldom corresponds with the Ideal, and often it happens that man, after many unsuccessful attempts to realise his ideals in the exterior world, returns to his interior world with disappoint- ment, and resolves to give up his search;

> *but if he succeeds in the realisation of his ideal, then arises for him a moment of happiness, during which time, as we know it, exists for him no more, the exterior world is then blended with his interior world, his consciousness is absorbed in the enjoyment of both, and yet he remains a man.*[26]

The reality is that with a lot of work and personal sacrifice 100's of thousands of individuals have accomplished a synchronicity from the internal and external world. One could be a CEO looking to innovate their business, a parent looking to strengthen the relationship with their children, or a prisoner with a dream to get his law degree and help others get their life together; all this is possible. Why can't you dream while working a minimum wage job, with no education, that you can be living in a 5,000 square foot mansion and a Lambo in your driveway? All it takes is a good sales job and a couple promotions and eventually starting a business with the learned skills.

Forget reality for a minute and let go of the myth that life is a constant struggle, luck is what happens when preparation meets opportunity.[27] Luck cannot be empirically predicted, but preparation and opportunity can 100% be controlled. The constant pursuit of the goal sets the foundation, and prepares us to receive the end-goal. The opportunity comes from putting ourselves in the proximity of those that can help us, that would buy from us, and with enough repetition of this cycle, there will be enough success for people to say, "we got lucky".

---

[26] Hartmann, Franz. Magic, White and Black. 1890, p. 46.
[27] Lucius Annaeus Seneca. Roman Stoic philosopher, statesman, dramatist, and humorist.

Exercise: External Vs Internal World

The intention of the exercise is to pinpoint where we are, and where we want to be. Below list the Top 6 current life situations you would like to change. Start where you are at and let your wildest fantasies take over. Forget reality and let you imagination show you the life you want. The point of this exercise is to determine the gaps and figure out how to realistically get there. How are you living? What is your life situation? How would you like things to be? Where do you see yourself? What's stopping you or what do you need to achieve it? What life do you truly desire?

	External World (Current Situation)	Internal World (Desired Reality)
1)		
2)		
3)		
4)		
5)		
6)		

Control Your Environment

Awareness, or being conscious, is to realize the elements in our life that slow us down or trap us in unnecessary cycles. That is the first step. The second is making sure we surround ourselves with the best environment to cultivate the "life" we want to live. Jordan Peterson says, *"if you want change, it starts with cleaning your room."* [28] If I want to be fit and have self-control issues, why would I keep junk food at home? At least make it harder to attain it. If "I can't make time," better organization, like meal prepping and pre-sorting supplements will cut hours of thinking and preparing each day. If "I can't seem to get out the door," prepare everything the night before to just wake up and walk out. Same applies for business or relationships, make it habit and systemize it in order to reduce as many variables that would lead to failure.

Just as we can be as efficient with our time, we have also discussed about taking away to let in what we want. This can include cutting people or activities from our life to get to where you need to be. Often times we have people in our life that have been there since the beginning of time, but not always in the best situations. We may have years of history and deep bonds with our past just to let it go like that; unfortunately, sometimes we have to if we want to grow. Once we open ourselves to a new way of life, once we done the work to toss our non-desired traits, and we are starting to see the results of our effort; someone from our past comes in to make us cheat, do drugs, or let our business go.

Not only are objects and places anchors or triggers to our past, so are people. Why is it that when we visit our

---

[28] Peterson, Jordan B. 12 Rules for Life: An Antidote to Chaos. Toronto, Vintage Canada, 16 Jan. 2018.

parents, we resort to a child-like dependency? Or when we meet with our drinking friends, all of sudden 1 drink turns to 16? Maybe we could be having a good day, but we get home to that juicy toxic relationship and hell breaks loose. The mere sight of that person makes our fight or flight instincts kick in. Why do we keep putting ourselves through this? I have lost many long-time friends, not due to disagreements, but because I was growing and they were stagnant. As we move to higher planes, if those around us do not want the same path, we can't force them to change and must move forward. This presents new challenges to those close to us, it is easier for them to put us down and keep us in the same place so their life can stay the same. Just because someone has been there our whole life, it does not mean that they will not be the ones trying to stop our progress when we decide to go in a new direction.

Personalize Your Journey

We don't need a designer belt, $200 pants, and a European sport car to park in a downtown high-rise to define our value. It also doesn't come from a mutated fake BBL rear-end or 20" arms. It comes from concocting, planning, and manifesting the life we always dreamed about through action. Some people dream of a quiet life on a farm, and others of a competitive profession and luxurious penthouse in downtown; both are in pursuit of life's desires. That is why worrying to meet the general mold is irrelevant, because we are here to pave our way and take what we like from what we have learned here. With this knowledge, it is up to us to differentiate those who have our best interest from those acting on self- interest. We control who we let in and we know who we need to cut off. Maybe a customer is causing you too many headaches, or a significant other is not contributing to our growth. Being polite shouldn't be mistaken for letting people into our life that do not fit our boundaries.

Actionable Steps

1) **Reflect on your life:** Observe your actions, thoughts, and emotions. Identify recurring patterns, limiting beliefs, and emotional triggers. Ask yourself "why?" until you reach the root, often buried in past experiences.

2) **Practice Mindfulness:** Become more aware of automatic responses and make conscious choices to challenge negative patterns and replacing them with desired actions. How do you want to be? Define your ideal future, then identify the gaps between your current reality and your aspirations.

3) **Design Your World:** Surround yourself and environment with positive influences that support your growth. Let go of relationships and situations that drag you down, even if it's difficult.

Summary:

This chapter is just the beginning of our journey to understanding and empowering our choices. As we delve deeper, remember: you are not a prisoner of your past; you are the author of your future.

1) Past experiences during childhood with parents, friends, family, educational institutions, social norms, and environment influence our present choices, beliefs and values.

2) Emotional triggers from past experiences and unconscious biases guide our decisions without our awareness.

3) We have the power to understand and overcome the limitations of our past.

4) Conscious effort and repetition help build new, empowering habits.

TAKE THE DRIVER SEAT:

Integrate Your Life.

> *"Your beliefs become your thoughts, your thoughts become*
> *your words, your words become your actions, your actions*
> *become your habits, your habits become your values, your*
> *values become your destiny."* [29]

> - Mahatma Gandhi

Summary: Grab life by the wheel and stop being a watcher from the
passenger seat. This chapter encourages self-awareness, proactive goal
setting, and consistent action to empower us to create the life we truly
desire. We delve into past influences shaping your present choices,
then work to design a dream life using specific goals in health, wealth,
relationships, and growth with the goal to build unshakeable
confidence through bold actions, clear communication, and self-
compassion. Each step deposits courage into our "confidence bank,"
boosting our power and presence. Finally, we learn to embrace our
authentic self, flaws and all, to attract the right people and live with
purpose. Remember, we are the architect of our journey. Take the
wheel and drive the life you deserve!

---

[29] Attributed to Mohandas Karamchand Gandhi, earlier version comes from
Marcus Aurelius meditations "Such as are thy habitual thoughts, such also will
be the character of thy mind; for the soul is dyed by the thoughts."

Take The Driver Seat

Imagine you are the car. For years we sat in the passenger seat while external forces dictated our direction. What if we were driving now? Where are we going? We discussed why we are stuck in the current situation and how to start making changes. This chapter is to understand why we do and want certain things, and how to take control of the way we do them.

Every action we take is either, moving us closer to our dream or further away, nothing stays at rest. The more actions we take towards our dream life and the more people we put ourselves in front of, result in more wins. As the wins start to avalanche, we operate at new higher vibrations, meet new connections, stumble upon opportunities; at the same time naturally alienating us from low frequency people or situations that don't serve us. The goal is to know what we want and having a set time-frame of when we will have it.

We want to paint a picture of the life we could be living and experience it in our mind, as if it was already happening because every action takes us closer to the realization of it. Just because life is momentarily in a bad part of a cycle, it does mean it is permanent. That reason things get better is the same reason things do not stay good. If everything is rhythm that flows with high and low tides, things that rise and fall; like the seasons or a pendulum, everything comes back full cycle. There's no reason to tolerate discomfort, unless It is chosen for a higher virtue; not because of passivity or fear.

"You are entitled to know that two entities occupy your body. One of these entities is motivated by and responds to the impulse of fear. The other is motivated by and responds to the impulse of faith.

Will you be guided by faith or will you allow fear to overtake you?"[30]

- Dale Carnegie

From Passenger to Pilot

Let's take the millions of successful people who have done this, from Rockefeller and Carnegie to Elon Musk and Jeff Bezos. These individuals had a "clear vision" about what they wanted, the preparation, and took action to be in the right place at the right time to create opportunities. It is not a magical law of attraction like *The Secret,*[31] where we sit around wishing away hopefully. That is part of the equation for when we are not working towards our goal, then we should be visualizing. A study referenced in *The Holographic Universe* by Michael Talbert[32] demonstrates that physical training provides almost equivalent results to rehearsing in the mind. The hidden component is about recreating the feeling and putting ourself in the scenario to act as if that was our life. We need to see it in first person as if we were there experiencing it, in color, listening to the sounds, feeling the feelings. Once we have the clear vision, it is about having a tangible plan and implement it. Become inspired by the end result and plan the step-by-step plan in reverse, from what we want to where we are at. So logical, common sense...why doesn't everyone have what they want already?

I do not think our goal in this lifetime is to waste 40 years living a cookie cutter life we were told to live just

---

[30] Carnegie, Dale. Outwitting the Devil: The Secret to Freedom and Success. New York, Sterling, 2018.

[31] Byrne, Rhonda. The Secret : The 10th Anniversary Edition. New York, Ny, Atria Books ; Hillsboro, Or, 2016.

[32] Talbot, Michael. The Holographic Universe. London Grafton Books, 1991.

realize one day that we are not happy, we hate our spouse, are miserable at our job but cannot leave; all our superficial friends and relationships only want to be around us if we conform to their whims. Now that we have some idea of where our previous life choices come from, we can take charge of the valuable years we have left. No matter how much time we have left, it always feels like too little. The more choices we have in life, we simultaneously feel more confident, we walk with a clear aim, we feel happy / excited / whole. We can be comfortable breaking superficial and unfulfilling relationships in our mission to really connect with those close to us. From a spiritual point of view, we are living our purpose. Whether we feel our strengths come from being a CEO or a housewife, we can still apply these principles to enrich our everyday life and add a new depth to the pursuit of living a purposeful life.

The Anchor Emotions

In the previous chapter we mentioned fear, anger, sadness, and guilt are some of the basic core emotions that drive negative perspectives and interpretations of the world. As we grow as human-animals we learn that fear and anger can be dissolved by learning, by understanding, by becoming more confident in what we believe. From that logic, we can exchange the past anger and understand that people that have wronged us were only doing what they thought was in their best interest, just as we would have.

Now, on our saddest day, whether we are on the diving board of suicide, or in the turmoil of a mental breakdown; it is us reacting to the emotions leaving us in a pit of uncertainty to engulf us in a lifeforce draining storm of negative thoughts. The funny part about these emotions is that they are momentary and we get over it. If we manage not to kill ourselves at that moment, we feel a little silly after. Whether it stems from situation or clinical depression, it is really just a momentary state of being. We surrender to our weakest most pitiful self and beg to be dead. So cliche. People wish they were dead because of trivial things like losing their jobs, failing a company, or the frozen yogurt place not having our favorite flavor. The funny part is that no matter how sad we are, the right person, event, condition, or any little thing will instantly shift our state. Staying sad is a protective shield against feeling sad again. We can shift it ourself in moments, but feeling happy feels foreign in these moments and only want to feel bad for ourselves.

The last one, to me is the easiest to understand, but the one that takes the most work. This is because it comes embedded within our programming to control us. Guilt is man-made. Pets do not feel guilty. If a dog eats a chicken, they are just acting in their nature. Guilt is used to stop us from sinning in religion, it could come from betraying someone's trust, or can come from something we did that we feel goes against our nature. That is real sin, going against our nature. Guilt can come from not abiding the label others put one us. One form of freedom comes from knowing that we are in control, with no restraint on who we can be and we cannot be. One example of breaking away from guilt is knowing that we do not have to feel bad or beg a boss to let us take a sick day or a vacation to spend time with family. We do not have to skip lunch because we had a phone call or an errand. We do not have to stop eating meat because our crazy girlfriend decided it was wrong. In later chapters we learn how selfishness can be a good thing and sadly, opening our eyes to the reality of the cut-throat world portrayed in *48 Laws of Power.*[33] The better we prepare for the manipulation and tricks of others during times of peace, the better we can see others masquerade

---

[33] Greene, Robert. The 48 Laws of Power. London, Profile, 2010.

when they have set their eyes on us as their target.

Unleash the Power Within

One thing millions learned during the 2-3 initial years of the "pandemic" is that priorities have changed. **There are four general areas in life which govern our whole existence: health, wealth, personal development, and relationship.** In the past career (wealth) was typically the highest importance for most. Before we may have felt guilty for leaving the office on-time. But once the plug was pulled and individuals were able to work from home and spend time with their growing children and pets, rather than commute for hours to be in an office all day and send their child to an industrialized learning facility. They were able to experience family like it once was, like how it was designed according to the American Dream. Suddenly that report did not matter because we were able to spend that extra commute time with our children, wife, pets, or whoever it may be. We realized that life balance is more important than surrendering our cherished ones for modern day slavery.

Exercise: Gap Analysis

List the things preventing you from achieving the goal using I-Statements (i.e. I waste two hours a day on my phone where I could be learning to invest).

Health:

Personal Growth:

Wealth:

Relationships:

Exercise: Gap Analysis - Part 2

List what you need to give up to achieve the goal in I-Statements (i.e. I need to stop going to the bar and spending $200 a weekend where that time and money could be allocated to my marketing budget and creating more content for my audience more).

Exercise: Gap Analysis - Part 2 (continue)

Health:

Personal Growth:

Wealth:

Relationships:

Integrate Your Life

Imagine the life; great health, financial freedom, fulfilling relationships, and the pursuit passions. This is not a fleeting wish; it is about crafting a detailed roadmap that excites and inspires us to build this ideal life. The fact that we can imagine a new life means we have the capability to make it happen. The ultimate goal is to beautify our lives and live a life in correspondence with our personal human nature, to maximize our experience here.

Now let's refine what would truly bring us satisfaction in each area of our life. One of the reasons why we are not living the life we want is because we do not know what we want and how good we can make things. To live a full life, we must maximize our creativity, curiosity, and the purpose of why we do things. We can take it a step further and actually map out the life we would like to be living that would give us aspirations for the future. It starts with little things like making our environment aesthetically pleasing to inspires us, refining our physical appearance to ensure we find beauty in ourselves and our body.

Health: foundation of everything, if our health is bad, we die; there are no more other areas. This could include diet, fitness, longevity goals.

Growth: wisdom, inspiration form religion, spirituality, meditation, personal development; it is about personal growth.

Wealth: set the foundation to live better, support our lifestyle, and help us be our best selves, to attract anything or anyone we want. Build generational wealth.

Relationships: they are what makes the whole thing tick, the flame to success. This includes family, significant others, close friends.

Exercise: Core Values

Step 1: List 15 qualities and traits that you would like to have in each area of your life (i.e. closer to family, quit drinking).

	Health	Growth	Wealth	Relationships
01)				
02)				
03)				
04)				
05)				
06)				
07)				
08)				
09)				
10)				
11)				
12)				
13)				
14)				
15)				

Step 2: Sort the 15 qualities and traits in order from most important (1) to least important (15) that you would like to have in each area of your life.

Exercise: Core Values (continue)

	Health	Growth	Wealth	Relationships
01)				
02)				
03)				
04)				
05)				
06)				
07)				
08)				
09)				
10)				
11)				
12)				
13)				
14)				
15)				

Step 3: List the top 5 most important qualities and traits to help define your ultimate purpose in each area.

	Health	Growth	Wealth	Relationships
01)				
02)				
03)				
04)				
05)				

Step 4: Construct "I" statements defining the ultimate goal for each area (i.e. I am 220lb at 12% bodyfat and inspire others to be their best self while making a living off fitness). Consider conflicts with the life we live now that need to go.

H:	
G:	
W:	
R:	

Building Belief

Now that we know our goals, it is time to pursue them. It might seem scary at times, but it only takes perseverance and belief. Achieving these goals is going to require belief in ourselves and taking levels of action we might have not put in before. That is what it takes to prove to the world that we mean business. Along the journey to our goals, we will develop additional life skills to help us further synergize our life with ease and build confidence in the process. Once the dust begins to settle, we start to see things clearly and we handle our basic human needs; we can start to move to the next level of healing and excelling.

This also ties to Maslow's hierarchy of needs[34], we have to satisfy our basic needs (physiological, safety, love and social, esteem, cognitive, aesthetic) so we can focus on our higher nature, spiritually or self-actualization. These are tools created by us humans to understand how to achieve higher levels of performance past mere survival. Many do not credit themselves because they cannot accept that they deserve a high-level position that they actually earned, but feel it was handed to them. We have to tell ourselves, "I

---

[34] Maslow, Abraham H. (1943). "A theory of human motivation". Psychological Review.

earned it" because we took care of the mere survival levels and transcended further to reach for our higher nature. The sad truth is that virtually all humans act on self-preservation. If we know where our choices come from, we can overcome our negative conditioning. The way we are programmed to treat our wife, parents, employees, etc., might not be the best way to do so. This may come from past programing and what we saw in our development. It is time to start making our own decisions.

Stages Of Character Evolution

We learned what matters to us most and what we need to do to maximize each area of our lives with the CORE VALUES exercise. Now it is time to determine what our ideal self would look like. Overflowing with this information, we can start to integrate those areas and implement the mindset to achieve it in real life. The logic of permanently becoming our best selves comes from starting to develop reasons to be "confident". Remember: *beliefs -> thoughts -> words -> actions -> habits -> values -> destiny.* We use our thoughts and past experiences to develop a foundation on what we think to be fact. When we know what we can do, it is time to start doing it and taking bold action. The more we repeat that bold action, we become more assertive and that becomes our new our habit. As time passes by, we being to build a foundational belief, or a conviction that we are this character.

Pay The Confidence Bank

Confidence [35] (noun) | con·fi·dence ˈkän-fə-dən(t) -ˌden(t)s

> **1a:** a feeling or consciousness of one's powers or of reliance on one's circumstances
> **b:** faith or belief that one will act in a right, proper, or effective way
> **2:** the quality or state of being certain : CERTITUDE
> they had every *confidence* of success

Confidence » Boldness » Assertiveness » Conviction

Being an expert means doing what we say we are going to do on command, it means being able to influence the world around us, and being able to create. It means having a deep knowing we do not lack the skills to successfully complete any task the world may throw at us. Expertise, regardless of skill or area of knowledge, mark us as someone with resources and with enough perseverance to plunge to depths of a subject. The crux of confidence is mastery. Mastery over something changes the way we feel and carry ourselves.

Picking up a new skill is like comparing a home garden we just started to an industrial farm producing crops to feed an entire city. After enough conscious practice, we start to develop a process and a sixth sense making the activity feel effortless, like those who have been doing it for years. Many books refer to this as "Flow." [36] Like everything in

---

[35] "Confidence." Merriam-Webster.com Dictionary, Merriam-Webster, https://www.merriam-webster.com/dictionary/confidence.

[36] Csikszentmihalyi, Mihaly. Flow: The Psychology of Optimal Experience. New York, Harper and Row, 1990.

life, we need to put in the conscious effort to grow to this point. As we are building external skills, we are also building the internal self-beliefs.

At times this challenges our internal patterns which are often shackled by limiting beliefs that attack our self-esteem (i.e., these are bad leads, it's management's fault). These limiting beliefs chip away at our self-worth, accomplishment, and respect. Others might get their self-esteem, or confidence from validation or status, but there still those that derive it from self-accomplishments. Esteem comes from reference experiences that provide the learning opportunities for us to discover ourselves, and realize our higher selves. These higher versions will require us to do things that are not common to us.

Forgiveness, compassion, empathy might not have been part of our vocabulary or focus; but accepting those things is something that will give us a feeling of self-respect, new strength, increased competence, mastery, self-confidence, independence, and freedom over ourselves. In the past we might have engaged in a profession or hobby just for the title or the recognition it gave us. This gave us a sense of contribution or value; this is also one example of how jobs capitalize on our loyalty. Ultimately, no matter the outcome, reason for doing it, or any other excuse; confidence comes from reference experiences which provide a learning opportunity that allows us to discover ourselves.

Stepping into Authenticity

Owning our true self with authority, including flaws, is the ultimate expression of personal power. To achieve this, we must let go of societal expectations and embrace our unique strengths, passions, and quirks. This vulnerability will not only attract the right people into our life but also liberate us to live with purpose and joy. The process to make a complete change comes in steps, but ultimately leads to our most ideal and powerful self. Power begins in the mind, if we feel confident and powerful, others feel it.

We typically can't go from starting a company to being a billionaire in an instant. It takes events and skills that build on the previous, and stack-on to help us reach the end goal. These reference experiences are what is going to build confidence in each area. In other words, the more experiences from action and skills we learn, the more reference experiences we have that provide proof to our subconscious that we have what it takes to be that new us.

As we build these, we begin to build a confidence bank which we can always reference for reasons and experiences to feel confident when times are hard. Confidence isn't built overnight; it's a steady journey. Each bold action contributes to our confidence bank. As we consistently practice these tools, a shift in perspective and actions begins to occur. We start to exude authority, command respect, and attract opportunity.

The Confidence Bank is something we build up like a point system; success builds on successes. This is what starts to build a confidence bank, which quickly turns to an unshakeable belief in ourselves. As a perfectionist, I am too aware of setting impossible and extremely ambitious goals that can rarely be meet, and this tends to cause confidence to degrade. Setting and accomplishing small goals at a time is key. When we know the benefit of something that we do regularly, we can confidently talk about why we are doing it, rather than if we do it out of habit. Often lack of confidence is associated with negative self-talk. Using our strengths to set and achieve small goals immediately stops negative words and replaces them with positive ones.

Quick Tips To Confidence:

❖ **Body Posture:** stand tall, sit up straight and move slow.

❖ **Eye Contact:** if you feel discomfort, focus on the color of people's eyes, or focus on the between the eyes as if staring thought them.

❖ **Tone:** speak relaxed, clearly, slowly with conviction. Use lower tone to appear more authoritative.

Exercise: Building A Confidence Bank:

What are you good at? Why do you do what do?

Part 1: List 15 strengths & positives that give you purpose and passion, that make you feel proud and confident about yourself.

01)	
02)	
03)	
04)	
05)	
06)	
07)	
08)	
09)	
10)	
11)	
12)	
13)	
14)	
15)	

Bold Action

Bold[37] (adjective) | ˈbōld

1a: fearless before danger:
INTREPID b: showing or requiring a
fearless daring spirit, a bold plan
5: ADVENTUROUS, FREE
6: standing out prominently

Confidence » **Boldness** » Assertiveness » Conviction

Break out of the comfort zone and take courageous steps to start challenging yourself, push boundaries, and cultivate inner strength. As the confidence bank builds, our actions become bolder. When we feel more confident, more of an authority figure, our responses and actions begin to shift. In the past we may have acted in a non-assertive way resulting in feeling less confident, leading to a self-reinforcing cycle of self-pity. By forcing ourselves to act confident and assertive, we begin to feel confident; therefore, reinforcing and strengthening our new set of beliefs we are building.

When we start pushing the boundaries, it might be a little like "fake it till you make it," but the more we act boldly, the more comfortable it feels. We enter everything with confidence knowing we are going to get it. This is a demonstration of our personal power commencing to shine. One thing to remember, use this power with kindness, respect, and dignity. As we get better at getting what we want, when we get what we want, it is very easy to step over others. One way to stay grounded is by mastering the techniques in Dale Carnegies,' "How to make friends

---

[37] "Bold." Merriam-Webster.com Dictionary, Merriam-Webster, https://www.merriam-webster.com/dictionary/bold. Accessed 15 Mar. 2023.

and influence people" [38] of asking questions and acting in the self-interest of others.

At this point in our journey, we may notice people react differently to us. This is the time to learn to express our needs and set our boundaries without being aggressive or overstepping others. This is a time to reflect on occasions where we have not communicated our wants and needs, and they have been trampled. What could we have done different? Are there times where we have done this to someone else? I bet they felt the same way we did. When we take care of our internal world with boldness and will, people start seeing us as someone that gets things done. Whether our specialty is in health (strength, physique), wealth (social status, influence), relationships (girlfriend/boyfriend, family, business partner), or Growth (expertise in a subject, religion); we want to be seen as someone who is able to take action, bold action, affect the world around us, and get people moving. Our partners want to know that we can influence outcomes, or hold authority over a subject with our mere word or intelligence. Who would have thought that our mind alone, armed with knowledge and expertise would be our biggest weapon against mediocrity and pre-set boundaries.

Quick Tips To Boldness:

❖ Take up space, powerful people take up space. This includes muscularity; it makes you physically bigger, thus taking up more space.

---

[38] Carnegie, Dale. How to Win Friends and Influence People. Harper Collins, 28 Jan. 2014.

❖ Start small talk with strangers, and observe their body language. Ask about them and talk about your interests in a captivating way that connects with them.

❖ Fake it, 'till you make it. Appear self-assured in every scenario even if you are not. Show that you don't share the doubts of others. Eventually you need to learn the skill, don't be all talk or it will misfire.

Exercise: Present You Vs New You

Recollect occasions where we have not been treated the way we think we deserve and how that situation should have looked like. If we know how situations should look like, we can start taking steps to making them look like that. Compare three (3) situations you are currently experiencing that you would like to change to the way you act. Whether this is a relationship, job, school, or fitness issue; list what you are currently doing and what would you would do if you took bold action?

	Present You	New You
1)		
2)		
3)		

Assertiveness Essentials

Assertive[39] (adjective) | as·ser·tive ə-ˈsər-tiv a-

Synonyms of assertive
1: disposed to or characterized by bold or confident statements and behavior

Confidence » Boldness » **Assertiveness** » Conviction

When we operate in a self-assured assertive manner, we begin to see new possibilities that may not have even crossed our mind before. We take riskier and bolder actions that leave people in awe, "how did you do that?" they will ask. The bolder action we take, that will be our new way of being and our belief will be strengthened. This gives us full conviction in our congruence. After all this, now we can call ourselves a confident person, and know it when anyone says, "just be yourself and be confident."

As we continue to refine our character, we start to take self-ownership of our life situation. We learned that acceptance of our past decisions and current temporary circumstances (career, relationships, physical) is key to not become engulfed in the worlds of others. It is time to emphasize our good qualities, address our flaws, and improve our appearance. It is time to trust ourselves and believe that we can handle any situation. We are adults, there is no longer a parent to patrol our every move. It is time to accept our mistakes without criticizing or labeling ourselves; and protect our beliefs, opinions, and ideas.

---

[39] "Assertive." Merriam-Webster.com Dictionary, Merriam-Webster, https://www.merriam-webster.com/dictionary/assertive.

Quick Tips To Assertiveness:

❖ **Control the Environment:** familiarity gives us a sense of control, making us feel confident, at ease, and powerful. Move things around, sit sideways on chairs, drape arms over the back, put your feet on the desk, this tells our subconscious we have control of our environment.

❖ **Be the Host:** what do you do when you have people over your house? Make others around you feel as comfortable as if they are in your home.

❖ **Ask Difficult questions:** ask personal questions without being intrusive, calibrate socially, be open with others, shift from "defensive mode" into "curiosity mode" while appearing confident.

From Timid Traveler to Fearless Explorer

Conviction[40] (Noun) | con·vic·tion kən-ˈvik-shən
2a: a strong persuasion or belief
b: the state of being convinced

Confidence » Boldness » Assertiveness » **Conviction**

Beliefs become thoughts, thoughts become actions, actions become habits. Our beliefs came from our past, and often self-generated from our environment. The previous exercises were meant to perform physiological actions that

---

[40] "Conviction." Merriam-Webster.com Dictionary, Merriam-Webster, https://www.merriam-webster.com/dictionary/conviction. Accessed 15 Mar. 2023.

would start to penetrate our psychology creating permanent change and a new destiny. Simultaneously, we might notice that we start to like ourselves more and more. We become convinced that we are worth it. We stop judging ourselves without a care about others' opinions, and simply face reality and what we want to improve on. We know ourselves better than someone who has only known us for a short period; therefore, our opinion about self is the only one that is relevant.

At this stage of growth, it is time to let go of anything that has not served us to be the person we ultimately want to be. At this stage we might also notice that our self-assurance gives us an irresistible aura drawing people in and making them want to get to know us. People might consider us their enemy because they are jealous, just dislike us for no reason, or some will passive-aggressively never complement us and secretly wish we fail. The way to be unphased by this is to have a solid knowledge of our abilities and who we are. Critiquing them will not do anything, if we focus on what we love, it will engage people who want to be around us.

Quick Tips To Conviction:

❖ **Live with Purpose:** pursuit something higher than yourself. Pick a cause, a goal, a vision and live it. We are alive to do something; we yearn for a cause, something greater than ourselves to believe in.

❖ **Own Yourself:** be okay with what you do and who you are now, no matter what that means. You can't do anything about it at this very moment. People like confident individuals, even if their other qualities are less attractive.

❖ **Be Flexible:** roll with the punches, be understanding but firm, don't contradict or push your beliefs on others.

❖ **Use Their Mask:** everyone is playing a role hiding their true self. Be aware and use the mask to your advantage. Life is short, embrace it and be free of the mask.

❖ **Live in Your Body:** fill up your whole body with spirit and presence to live in it entirely.

Exercise: Strengths and Weaknesses

List your strengths and weaknesses. Work on your weaknesses until they're minimal. Read it daily until you are sure that what you wrote down are your real abilities and skills. When someone criticizes or labels you, see if what they said matches your judgment of yourself. If it doesn't then it doesn't matter; if it does, then they just helped you discover one more thing to work on.

	Strengths:
01)	
02)	
03)	
04)	
05)	
06)	
	Weaknesses:
01)	
02)	
03)	
04)	
05)	
06)	

Summary:

This chapter outlines a framework for taking control of our life and achieving our desired outcomes. It emphasizes the importance of understanding our past influences, setting clear goals, and developing confidence through consistent action.

1) **Past Influences:** Our current choices and perspectives are shaped by our past experiences, environment, and upbringing. Recognizing these influences allows us to break free from limiting patterns.

2) **Goal Setting:** Define core values in life across different areas like health, wealth, relationships, and personal growth. Create a vision for your ideal self and the life you want to live.

3) **Building Belief:** Develop belief in yourself and your ability to achieve your goals through "bold action" overcoming fears, negativity, and limiting beliefs.

4) **Stages of Character Evolution:** This framework outlines four stages of personal growth: Confidence, Boldness, Assertiveness, and Conviction. Each stage builds upon the last, leading to a powerful and self-assured version of yourself.

5) **Taking Action:** Consistent intentional action is essential for building confidence, self-worth, and achieving goals. The chapter provides practical tips for developing assertive body language, communication, and self-presentation.

6) **Living with Purpose:** Find a higher purpose or cause that motivates you and gives your life meaning. This adds depth and fulfillment to your journey.

7) **Owning Yourself:** Embrace who you are and what you do, regardless of others' opinions. True power comes from self-understanding, living with purpose, and embracing your authentic self in accordance with your values.

SELFISH IS GOOD

What do you really want?

"It never ceases to amaze me: we all love ourselves more than other people, but care more about their opinion than our own." [41]

- Marcus Aurelius

Summary: Labels, both praise and criticism, box us in. Stop listening! Discover the real "you" by defying limitations and prioritizing desires. It's okay to be "selfish"; prioritize your well-being, set boundaries, and stop being a pushover. Craft your dream life, not someone else's. You radiate power when you authentically connect with others and inspire their own growth. Take the wheel of your life! Envision your ideal self and commit to the journey. It's time to ditch the labels and unlock your authentic, empowered potential.

---

[41] Aurelius, Marcus. Meditations. Penguin, 2019.

Labels Put Us In A Box

Any label, whether positive or negative, influences our behavior. A study from "Encyclopedia of Human Behavior" determined that:

> *...our beliefs about others can lead us to treat them in such a way that they subsequently become what we expect them to be. Originally, the effect was demonstrated in the classroom and called the 'pygmalion effect.' In a seminal study, teachers were told at the beginning of a school year that certain of their students were potential late bloomers, who would be expected to excel during the school year under proper guidance. Even though there was nothing in actual fact that set those students apart from their colleagues, several months later their schoolwork had improved considerably.* [42]

This created a self-fulfilling philosophy resulting in better grades, the teacher gave the students the label and internalized just like we do daily. A partner might call us narcissistic, controlling or insecure if we complain about promiscuous behavior; this to make us comply and accept the behavior, or agree that we are that label. A manager might put us down and say things like, "remember, I got you this position" or "what would you do without me?"; this is, of course, to create an inferiority and dependency. The manager is labeling us as their inferior and that we are less capable than them. Begin by no longer listening to peoples' words, and look at their intention. Determine if the label is for our betterment or to attempt to manipulate us to act a certain way in order to not fall under the label

---

[42] Ramachandran, Vilayanur S. Encyclopedia of Human Behavior. 2nd ed., Amsterdam ; Heidelberg, Academic Press, 2012, pp. 410–417.

they have set. Labels are starting to sound like a spell or curse, depending on who said it, that can actually control our behavior or environment. Everyone operates on self-interest. If our boss tells us that we are one of his top employees on the way to the promotion, we act differently than if we were at a dead-end-job. Later we find out that he told that to everyone, and someone outperformed us and were promoted. The extra hours, long weekends, and missed time with family all seems pointless, the label of "top employee" is no longer there to drive us.

Using words to manipulate others may seem very enticing at this point. I mean, sometimes the bad guys seem to be having all the fun, but so do the good guys who follow their own rules. Think of an anti-hero or misanthrope like Hannibal Lecter or Deadpool, they're essentially good people in an environment that made them to resort to gray area behavior to survive, while doing their form of good. If we continue to live to a "standard" or "label" we run the risk of never fully realizing our full potential. These individuals who reached the stage Übermensch,[43] those who crosses the threshold in their Heroes Journey,[44] or who reached self-actualization according to Maslow.[45] The desire to become everything that we could become, that is the goal of those who are ambitious. But it is not just ambition, it the calling of the soul.

---

[43] Frederich Nietzsche. Thus Spake Zarathustra. 2019.
[44] Campbell, Joseph. The Hero with a Thousand Faces : A Brilliant Examination, through Ancient Hero Myths, of Man's Eternal Struggle for Identity. Nueva York, Fontana Press, 1949.
[45] Maslow, Abraham H. (1943). "A theory of human motivation". Psychological Review.

Break Free From Labels

As the hero of our lives, it is up to us to question and reject labels we carelessly accepted in the past. When something does not resonate, challenge it. Labels often reflect the labelers' insecurities, not ours. Don't let them control our actions or define our worth. For example, in a relationship or job, they can be imposed over such a long period that we eventually begin to embody them. Labels to put us in a box are projections of the accuser to break us down. The more we start to change and work on ourselves, expect resistance. As we change and grow, it will be a threat to those around us and our confidence will be challenged. They will attack us various ways to try to put us back in the box where we were easily controlled. If they are satisfied with our actions, they tell us we are a good person; if not, they may continue to label us anything that suits their faulty perception in order to continue manipulate us.

One of their goals is to create self-doubt and make us question if we are making the right choices, or we are actually perceiving the situation as it really is. This a form of "gaslighting." [46] For example, a boss might tell us if you leave the industry, don't put in the long hours, or don't hook up with him; you will never be able to find a job again. This might come up in a relationship. A partner might see that we are starting to better ourselves, but they do not want to change their life. One route is to grow with us. The other is to tell us, "You're perfect as you are," "you don't have to work out," or "you're neglecting the relationship by going

---

[46] Conrad, Marissa. "What Is Gaslighting? Meaning, Examples and Support." Forbes Health, 17 Mar. 2022, www.forbes.com/health/mind/what-is-gaslighting/#:~:text=To%20gaslight%20someone%20means%20to.

a form of psychological manipulation that hinges on creating self-doubt...It's making someone seem or feel unstable, irrational and not credible, making them feel like what they're seeing or experiencing isn't real, that they're making it up, that no one else will believe them.

back to school"; ultimately, whether consciously or unconsciously they are trying to hold us back because they are scared that once we improve our lives, we will no longer depend on them, or expect something better. Ideally there should not have been dependency to begin with, but we messed up and chose the wrong environment.

Now being aware, we are free to liberate our choices, through the elimination of acting within the boundaries set by others' opinions, in an attempt to define our position within their world. Those around us will continue to label us. Welcome these labels and laugh, add them to a list and see how these compare to our actual beliefs. We are no longer the person who leaves the decision to others tell us who we are.

Love Who You Are, What You Do, And What You Look Like

We constantly compare ourselves to others; to make it worse, we choose criteria we are already weak at, putting us on the losing side. We ignore all the greatness about us and pick on the one flaw we lack to compare it to others.

Exercise: Brutal Reality

Who is labeling you? What are they labeling you? When/Where/Why are they labeling you that (what do they have to gain)?

Who?	What?	When / Where / Why?
Parent		
Spouse		
Child		
Boss		
Friends		
Others		

Reclaiming Selfishness, It's All About Me

I don't know about you, but I am a little angry that everyone I thought cared about me has been manipulating me this whole time. What do we do? Rebel against them or hurt them? Ignore it because we love them or want to keep our jobs? The real question is, if you knew someone you loved was being taken advantage off or abused what would you do? What would you do if your child was getting bullied, your elderly mom was being harassed by the landlord, or you wife constantly being hit on by the boss? Why let someone do that to us? After doing all this work on

71

ourselves, it might start feeling like we should only be concerned about us, or we might feel some animosity toward those manipulating us.

The reality is that we have been allowing it, and all we can do is take control, make our own conscious decisions. This might involve taking some time away to reassess the relationship, or it might mean cutting off or permanently reducing the time we spend with someone. This might seem selfish, but the better person we are, the better we can be for those we care about. The key is to selfishly love ourselves so it spills over to everything else. Prioritize physical, mental, and emotional well-being. It's not selfish, it is essential. Set boundaries, don't let work exploit us, maintain financial spending limits with our spouse, prioritize self-care, reassess relationships that drain us. Are you giving more than you receive? Is it worth it?

Personal profit will spill-over to those around us. Some will accuse us, "you changed," "you're mean now," "you don't spend as much time with me, I don't feel like you love me," "are you depressed? I haven't seen you at the bar," this is to pull the aversion of the previous trigger words to manipulate us back to who we were. Everyone around is driven by different motivators, but anytime we are not predictable and safe for their reality, it is time to start labeling. If we do not take care of our physical, mental and emotional health, we cannot perform at our best. It is about our boundaries with our friends, family, and partners. They should understand if they really have our wellbeing in mind.

Lack of Boundary Enforcement:

❖ Watching others get promoted while keeping you as the go-to person who spends the extra hours at work.

❖ Your wife treats you like a credit card while doing the bare minimum to take care of you.

❖ Spending past what's comfortable to continue to do activities to keep up with you friends.

These are instances in relationships that need to be reassessed. Are we giving so much of ourselves that we are too drained to pursue our hobbies or higher work? Is the return at least worth it? Does putting the long hours ensure we'll never get skipped for a promotion? Will supporting the household stop a spouse from cheating? Are all the memories going to force our friends to be there when we really need someone?

Previously:

Selfish [47] (adjective) | self·ish ˈsel-fish

Synonyms of *selfish*
1: concerned excessively or exclusively with oneself : seeking or concentrating on one's own advantage, pleasure, or well-being without regard for others
2: arising from concern with one's own welfare or advantage in disregard of others
a *selfish* act

[47] "Selfish." Merriam-Webster.com Dictionary, Merriam-Webster, https://www.merriam-webster.com/dictionary/selfish. Accessed 11 Jan. 2024.

Redefined:

Selfish2 (adjective) | self·ish 'sel-fish

1: concerned excessively or exclusively with oneself: seeking or concentrating on one's own advantage, pleasure, or well-being with the purpose to be the best self for others

Define Your Own Path, What Do You Really Want?

If we are not our upbringing, and we are not the expectations of those closest to us, then what are we? It seems there was never a set way to be, and what we thought was the cookie-cutter norm, was actually a suggestion of the path set forth by the pioneers who were out there "figuring it out," we can call this a tradition. Just like the early pioneers, it is up to us to define our own norm and figure out what we want to pass on to the next generations.

We can work a job where we wake up every morning hoping something happens to not go in, or we can wake up exited to make a difference in the world in the pursuit of our higher calling. Knowing what we want and what we will allow, we can maneuver effortlessly in this stage called Life. Others will sense the confidence and feel assured. We become a source of pleasure without being a pushover or people pleaser. When we have a conversation, we inspire and make others feel like the most important person in the room. As they get lost in conversation about their desires, passions and aspirations; we listen genuinely and leave them walking away more confident and excited about themselves. I know the external world does not match our internal world yet, but we can dream. It is time to outline what our perfect life looks like and who we need to be to thrive in that life. If we want to add horsepower to a car, we can upgrade the engine; the driver of our body (vessel) can work out to make it stronger. If we don't like how it looks externally, we can paint the car, just like how we can put on new clothes. Is the environment harming our car? We can move it too. That is the level of power and control we have over ourselves. It is time to choose the life we want to live and the person we want to be while living it.

Boundary Setting

1) We have the right to our own values, beliefs, opinions, and emotions.

2) We do not have to justify or explain our actions to others.

3) We have the right to be treated with respect, and tell others how we expect to be treated.

4) We have the right to express our thoughts, and say, "No," "I don't know," "I don't understand," and "I don't care."

5) We have the right to make mistakes.

Exercise: Character Avatar

Visualize the ideal life. What does it look like? Who are you in it? This is the start of the journey. Based on all the previous exercises, we have a good grasp on how our ideal "higher" self would look. Someone we would have looked up to as a child. Rethink how life could be and the person we would need to become to make the external match the internal.

I call this exercise the "Metal Man Suit" because I do not want to get sued for copyright. The "Metal Man Suit" concept is an exercise for us to construct our own "Ideal Self" avatar and walk into it as we go out into the world. Think of it as an upgrade to our "vessel". Based on all the previous values exercises, create scenarios and determine how this Ideal Self would act in these instances until it is no longer a suit we wear, but has become part of us.

Summary:

This chapter reviews that labels can limit us and encourages taking control of our lives by prioritizing our own desires and setting healthy boundaries.

1) **Labels influence behavior:** Stop accepting labels others put on us, as they limit our potential.

2) **Question motivations:** Recognize that everyone acts in their own self-interest and challenge manipulative labels.

3) **Be comfortable in our own skin:** Embrace our authentic self and resist pressure to conform.

4) **Prioritize self-love:** Take care of our physical, mental, and emotional well-being.

5) **Set healthy boundaries:** Don't let others drain our energy or exploit us.

6) **Define our own "norm":** Don't follow someone's path; design the ideal life.

7) **Empower ourselves and others:** Focus on personal growth and inspiring others.

PLAN TO WIN

One Action Every Moment.

"The journey of a thousand miles begins with a single step."[48]

- Lao Tzu

Summary: Unleash your power by breaking free from programmed patterns and challenge your routines. You're grinding DAY-BY-DAY for your goals; a planner is the way to keep score. Build your action roadmap using tools like daily planners, hyper-focus blocks, and SMART goals. Check off tasks as accomplishments to track progress and prioritize. Become a laser-focused achiever, small actions fueled by intention and repetition lead to big victories!

---

[48] Laozi, and D C Lau. Tao Te Ching. London, Penguin, 2003.

Unlock The Power Plan

We're not trapped in a cycle of reacting to circumstances. Every action triggers an equal reaction, a cause and effect empowering us to shape our path. We often know what to do, but sticking to it is the challenge. As humans, we operate on patterns, not far from intelligent animals. Recognizing our patterns is key to breaking free and achieving our desired reality. When we know what we want, and what we need to do to get it, we usually do it if we want it want bad enough. When we catch our previously unconscious patterns, we start see what is preventing us from achieving our desired external world situation.

The first step is to start separating our current choices from patterns we have continually followed. Look around at people who act different than us and try to understand why? Look at their communities and how they differ than ours. Now look at the communities we associate with and compare their actions to ours, do we act like everyone else? Notice, we too have been absorbed by the machine. The more we notice what is genuine "us" and what is our persona, we begin to see the influence of our programming.

We absorb energy just being around anything too long. With this fact, now we can begin to calibrate our behaviors. Eating a whole cake before bed when we are trying to lose weight, or staying out drinking all night when we are trying to fix our marriage is not the solution. Through daily actionable task, we design a way to make progress toward a goal. This tool is built to give us a canvas to paint our new life and create a roadmap to get there. It is a way to stop others from draining us in our environment and maximizing the energy we can focus on improving our life. No longer will others be able to labels us and try to guilt us to take our power. They also will not be able to play off our emotions, and deviate us from our path; because our path is our mission, and we are helping those we love by pursuing it. Whether our goal is to leave a trust fund for our family to continue to grow over the generation, or become an astronaut, there is a roadmap to get there.

Daily Planner, The Command Center

Later in this chapter we look into creating a roadmap for our goals and planning our year with actionable items. All this starts with daily actions. If our ideal health goal is to lose 60-pounds in a year, then we probably want to be 30 pounds lighter by mid-year, and we would also want to keep track that we are losing 5-pounds a month. Those would be milestones described in the SMART Goals and Action Plan section. Along with the monthly plan of losing 5-pounds a week, we need to track weekly and daily actions like, exercising 3 times a week for 1-hour and eating 4 healthy meals a day.

Top Activities to Track:

❖ **Top 5 Tasks:** Tackle the toughest first! Completing difficult tasks early boosts productivity and mood.

❖ **Daily To-Do List:** Categorize tasks (computer, office) for clearer organization thought your day.

❖ **Goals/Wins:** Celebrate achievements with small rewards, big or small, to stay motivated.

❖ **Next Day Plan:** Set priorities for tomorrow to avoid decision fatigue.

❖ **End of Day Summary:** Reflect on progress and identify areas for improvement.

❖ **Meditated? (Yes/No):** Prioritize mindfulness – research shows it reduces stress and improves focus.[49]

Morning Questions / Reflection:

❖ **Gratitude:** What am I grateful for? Gratitude can rewire the brain for positivity, fueling motivation.

❖ **Progress:** What good shall I do today? Nurture a growth mindset and always look for opportunities to help.

❖ **Challenge:** How will I challenge myself today? Step outside your comfort zone daily, it fosters growth and resilience.

❖ **Excitement:** What am I excited about today? Anticipation fuels action! Identify something to look forward to each day.

❖ **Inspiration:** How will I inspire and motivate others? Be the change, seek out to be a role model to keep your fire burning.

---

[49] "A Beginner's Guide to Meditation." Mayo Clinic, 14 Dec. 2023, www.mayoclinic.org/tests-procedures/meditation/in-depth/meditation/art-20045858#:~:text=Meditation%20can%20help%20you%20relax.

Example: Daily Planner

WEEKLY GOAL:		DATE: _____
TIME	**ACTIVITY**	**TOP 5 TASKS**
04:00		1
05:00		2
06:00		3
07:00		4
08:00		5
09:00		
10:00		**TO DO LIST (A/C)**
11:00		
12:00		
13:00		
14:00		
15:00		
16:00		
17:00		
18:00		
19:00		
20:00		
21:00		
22:00		
23:00		
24:00		**NOTES**

Hyper-Focus Blocks

Distractions are productivity killers. The Pomodoro Technique[50] (25-minute work block followed by 5-minute breaks) is a popular solution and works synergistically with "hyper-focus blocks" dedicating a time block to specific life areas. The Pomodoro technique typically calls for four (4) of these 25/5-minute blocks, followed by a longer 20-minute break. This allows us to block time for life sectors like health (morning workout) or learning (evening reading). To take it further, Grant Cardone[51] suggests to try to do as much as you can in 15-minutes by setting a timer. This forces us to race against ourselves. Elon Musk takes it a step further and suggests he uses 5-minute increments. Apply the Hyper-Focus Block tool to each life sector. Schedule a morning workout block or an evening reading block. For example, we can block from 5:00am to 6:30am dedicated to health which could include meditating, stretching and a workout.

Getting Things Done:[52] Declutter the Mind

This is a game-changer system and book by David Allen to help clear our mind of tasks and projects, and allow for full focus on the task at hand. Instead of carrying mental burdens of open projects and due dates, Getting Things Done (GTD) takes the open tasks, projects, and information out of our mind and onto a digital/written tool to categorizing them in "buckets" based on type, location and due date.

---

[50] Cirillo, Francesco, The Pomodoro Technique, archived from the original on 31 March 2023

[51] "The Official Website of Grant Cardone." Grant Cardone - 10X Your Business and Life, 14 June 2018, grantcardone.com/.

[52] Allen, David (2015). Getting Things Done: The Art of Stress-Free Productivity (2 ed.). Penguin Books. ISBN 9780143126560.

Benjamin Franklin Daily Schedule[58]

Learn from the master! Explore Benjamin Franklin's daily schedule for inspiration on structuring our day for max productivity.

The morning question, What good shall I do this day?	5	Rise, wash, and address *Powerful Goodness;* contrive day's business and take the resolution of the day; prosecute the present study; and breakfast.
	6	
	7	
	8	
	9	Work.
	10	
	11	
	12	Read or overlook my accounts, and dine.
	1	
	2	
	3	Work.
	4	
	5	
	6	Put things in their places, supper, music, or diversion, or conversation; examination of the day.
	7	
	8	
	9	
Evening question, What good have I done today?	10	
	11	
	12	
	1	Sleep.
	2	
	3	
	4	

---

[58] https://www.theatlantic.com/politics/archive/2011/04/picture-of-the-day-benjamin-franklins-daily-schedule/237615/

SMART Goals

SMART is an acronym for a goal-setting system first proposed by George T. Doran[54] to facilitate the evaluation of progress in the pursuit of a clear expected outcome. This tool applies across various life areas or sector such as business, health, or relationships.

[S] Specific: simple, not a detailed list of how to meet a goal; the mission statement of goal. Use active words like "coordinate," "create," "implement;" and avoid words like "improve," "reduce," "increase" (e.g. "reduce cost"). These focus on the direction, but don't explain specific action.

❖ What will you achieve?

❖ Who is involved?

❖ Where is it located?

❖ What actions will you take?

> **Example:** *I had a bad sales quarter during my performance review. I need to meet a X% close rate and find X new customers a week. This needs to be implemented by next quarter (3-months) for my review.*

[M] Measurable: meaningful and motivating metrics to determine if the goal is met. Measure progress and set milestones for tasks and steps along the way; when we add up the result, it should lead to the completion of the goal.

---

[54] Doran, G. T. (1981). "There's a S.M.A.R.T. way to write management's goals and objectives" (PDF). Management Review. 70 (11): 35–36.

❖ How will data be captured to determine when the goal is met? Quantitative (productivity results, money saved or earned) and qualitative (client testimonials, surveys).

❖ What data will measure the goal? How much? How well? How many?

❖ Data types and data collection methods may include:

- Quality/accuracy rates
- Revenue generated
- Surveys
- Productivity rates
- Products, samples
- Customer Satisfaction

Example: *By my quarter review, I will have contacted X new customers a week in order to meet the end goal of XX. I will establish a baseline where I am currently at and chart my outreach rate, conversion and close rate.*

[A] Achievable: what can you do to make it attainable, may require new skills and changing attitudes. Consider what you have control over, and what others do. If you want a promotion, it is up to the boss. We can only control the preparation we take for the position.

❖ How can I accomplish this goal, is the goal doable?

❖ How realistic is the goal, based on constraints such as finance and time?

❖ Are you sure you can do this? Do you have the skills and resources; if not, what would it take to attain them?

Example: *My job depends on meeting my sales goal. I will set time to for sales courses and daily sales training to improve my close rate. I will also look for new sources of leads to find new customers.*

[R] Relevant: reasonable, realistic and a resource to other areas.

❖ Does this seem worthwhile?

❖ Is this the right time?

❖ Does this match our other efforts/needs?

❖ Is it applicable in the socio-economic environment?

❖ Does the goal align with the team or organization?

❖ How will the result matter?

Example: *Meeting the sales goal is 85% of my job. As I move up in the company, I will need to make sure my whole team can meet their sales goal. I can use the new skill on any position I work in the future.*

[T] Time: time based, target date for deliverables, deadline and what can be accomplished within that time period.

❖ What is the deadline for accomplishing the goal?

❖ What should be achieved half-way through the process?

❖ What can I do six months from now?

❖   What can I do six weeks from now?

❖   What can I do today?

> **Example:** *In 3-months, I should have increased my close rate by X% and have X new customers a week.*

SMART Goal Example:

> *To continue in and grow in my career, I need to meet a set close rate and develop new lead avenues. By taking classes and daily training, I will improve my close rate by X%. Additionally, by exploring new lead sources, I will meet with X new customers a week.*

Milestone: *Complete sales course and continue daily training, also explore new lead sources in the next 3-months.*

Deadline: *quarterly review in 3-months.*

Exercise: SMART Goals

Step 4: Construct a SMART Goal for each life area. Is there any conflict with the life you live now that you need to let go?

HEALTH SMART Goal:

[S]:

[M]:

[A]:

[R]:

[T]:

GROWTH SMART Goal:

[S]:

[M]:

[A]:

[R]:

[T]:

Exercise: SMART Goals (continue)

	WEALTH SMART Goal:
[S]:	
[M]:	
[A]:	
[R]:	
[T]:	
	RELATIONSHIP SMART Goal:
[S]:	
[M]:	
[A]:	
[R]:	
[T]:	

Action Plan, Our Personal Roadmap to Greatness

Do we get dressed, jump in our car and leave our home without knowing where we are headed? Armed with a clearly mapped SMART goal, it is time to hit the pavement running. Nothing left but to make a gameplan and start chipping away at the larger goal. Remember, consistency is key. If you're setting a goal and acting, it could actually come true. What are you going to do when it does? And how is life going to be when you have it? All these things can, and will happen. If we think about the goal in a way where we expect it to happen, and have a clear idea of how it is going to be when we have it, it will motivate us to act as if it is in progress. That will influence us to make choices based on that new reality.

Additional Tips:

1) Find an accountability partner for support.

2) Embrace setbacks as learning opportunities.

3) Celebrate your progress.

Exercise: Create An Action Plan

Step 5: We spoke about creating an **action plan** earlier in this book in order to have a clear step-by-step set of actions that we can peruse each day, and know that we are one step closer to our goal. Write a step-by-step breakdown about how to get to be where you want to be. List the **Daily** and **Weekly** actions you MUST take to achieve the goal, and list any other action you need to track. Think about this as a cheat sheet when you are unsure on what comes next, or you had an exceptionally bad day.

Exercise: Create An Action Plan (continue)

HEALTH Actions To Achieve Goal:
1)
2)
3)
4)
5)
6)

GROWTH Actions To Achieve Goal:
1)
2)
3)
4)
5)
6)

Exercise: Create An Action Plan (continue)

WEALTH Actions To Achieve Goal:

1)

2)

3)

4)

5)

6)

RELATIONSHIP Actions To Achieve Goal:

1)

2)

3)

4)

5)

6)

Exercise: Plan The Year, Quarter, Month, Week, Day

This exercise like a "Pyramid Set" in bodybuilding. This where we start with a lighter weight (short tern: 3-month from now). Then we gradually increase the weigh until we can only do 6-repetitions (5-year goal).

3-Month Goals:
[H]:
[G]:
[W]:
[R]:

6-Month Goals:
[H]:
[G]:
[W]:
[R]:

1-Year Goals:
[H]:
[G]:
[W]:
[R]:

5-Year Goals:
[H]:
[G]:
[W]:
[R]:

Exercise: Plan The Year, Quarter, Month, Week, Day (continue)

Usually during pyramid sets, we realize how light the weight previously was as we are dropping weight each set. When we are going backwards, we may realize we were limiting what we could do in that amount of time.

	5-Year Goals:
[H]:	
[G]:	
[W]:	
[R]:	

	1-Year Goals:
[H]:	
[G]:	
[W]:	
[R]:	

	6-Month Goals:
[H]:	
[G]:	
[W]:	
[R]:	

	3-Month Goals:
[H]:	
[G]:	
[W]:	
[R]:	

Summary:

1) We have the power of choice and to take responsibility for our actions.

2) We have the ability to move from reacting to circumstances, to creating our path.

3) Learn to recognize and break limiting patterns.

4) Understand the importance of a roadmap for achieving goals.

5) Review and apply your SMART-goals and step-by-step action plan daily.

6) Set deadlines and milestones.

REVISIT YOUR LIFE

Playful Action Fuels Happiness.

"The cave you fear to enter holds the treasure you seek." [55]

- Joseph Campbel

Summary: After going through this journey, you have become a new person. You probably knew that the person that started this planner would not remain the same, but now it is your time to reassess your cause and start again another year. Conscious introspection leads to action, embrace life's challenges with a light heart and detach from worst-case scenarios. Focus on desired outcomes, cultivate a positive outlook, and set healthy boundaries. Don't demand, collaborate! Request things that align with others' best interests for mutual success. Revisit your core values and ensure your daily choices reflect them. Take proactive steps to move closer to your vision. Remember, life is a playground, and a battlefield. Play boldly, act purposefully, and fuel your happiness!

---

[55] Campbell, Joseph. The Hero with a Thousand Faces : A Brilliant Examination, through Ancient Hero Myths, of Man's Eternal Struggle for Identity. Nueva York, Fontana Press, 1949.

What's Next?

Welcome to the end of this transformative journey! We have explored our values, passions, and current reality; it's time to transform awareness into action. Remember, life is a playground and a battlefield. Let's embrace a playful, yet determined spirit as we move forward. Closing this planner means it is time to open it again as we realize we're not the same person who began it. It's time to reflect on growth, revisit our goals, and chart a course for the year ahead.

After consciously reviewing all aspects of life, it is time to take it by the reigns. If you want it, take it. The only way to win is to play the game of life. We need to take a light-hearted approach and keep moving forward. Becoming a social chameleon is part of mastering CHARM, but only after mastering oneself will this free us to no longer lose ourselves to fit in the group. Sadly, we often conform to group norms rejecting our authentic selves and taking a knee on our beliefs because we fear rejection or missing out. More times than not, it is when we accept ourselves and tap into our childhood inclinations that we discover that which truly fulfils us. Serving others' labels no longer serve us because we are too busy perusing our natural inclinations. No longer are we trying to please others, we are driven by a force to grow, to be our best selves for ourselves and those we love. Robert Greene states:

> *"In order to master a field, you must love the subject and feel a profound connection to it. Your interest must transcend the field itself and border on the religious."* [56]

> *- Robert Greene*

---

[56] Greene, Robert. Mastery. New York, New York, Penguin Books, 2013, p. 298.

Ikigai, The Meaning of Life

We've all heard "follow your passion," but how do we pay the bills? One philosophy that attempts to explain the meaning of life is the Japanese concept of Ikigai. This philosophy combines a feeling of delight and peace focused on the present knowns as *shiawase.* This is closely related to hedonic well-being, or hedonia; which is immediate sensory pleasure, happiness, and enjoyment. The second is feeling *ikigai,* we achieve this through devoting ourselves to pursuit what we enjoy; giving us the feeling of accomplishment and fulfillment. This includes awareness of our values, purpose of life, and meaning of existence. It is future oriented such as goal seeking. Ikigai is close to *eudaimonic* well-being, the consequences of self-growth and self-actualization.[57] Basically, feeling good on the outside and inside.

---

[57] Kumano, Michiko. "On the Concept of Well-Being in Japan: Feeling Shiawase as Hedonic Well-Being and Feeling Ikigai as Eudaimonic Well-Being." Applied Research in Quality of Life, vol. 13, no.2, 9 May 2017, pp. 419–433, https://doi.org/10.1007/s11482-017-9532-9.

Confronting Worst-Case Scenarios

Achieving Ikigai sounds like a heaven on earth and cultivating a positive mindset requires effort, but the rewards are immense.

As we move forward setting clear boundaries to protect our well-being, we will still have bad days. On our worst days, all we can do is look at the worst possible outcome, hope for the best, and not to dwell on it. Detach emotionally from it, with full acceptance, and charge forward with hope of the best. This is an act of acknowledging, then releasing, in order to move forward with clarity and newfound courage. Ultimately, the goal is to feed the outcome, not the situation. Life is hard enough as it is, why make it harder? Maintaining a pleasant feeling takes work, why make it harder by getting involved in the unnecessary stressors. Let's set boundaries from the beginning moving forward. Let's work with others and request things in a way that make them feel like mutual self-interest for both parties so they actually do them.

Exercise: Core Values - Revisit Our Life to Align Values with Actions

Now is the time to revisit your core values and ensure your actions reflect them. Values create your actions.

❖ How do my daily choices align with my values?

❖ Are there areas where I can make adjustments to live more authentic?

❖ What specific actions can I take today to move closer to my vision?

Step 1: List 15 qualities and traits that you would like to have in each area of your life (i.e. closer to family, quit drinking).

	Health	Growth	Wealth	Relationships
01)				
02)				
03)				
04)				
05)				
06)				
07)				
08)				
09)				
10)				
11)				
12)				
13)				
14)				
15)				

Step 2: Sort the 15 qualities and traits in order from most important (1) to least important (15) that you would like to have in each area of your life.

	Health	Growth	Wealth	Relationships
01)				
02)				
03)				
04)				
05)				
06)				
07)				
08)				
09)				
10)				
11)				
12)				
13)				
14)				
15)				

Step 3: List the top 5 most important qualities and traits to help define your ultimate aim in each area.

	Health	Growth	Wealth	Relationships
01)				
02)				
03)				
04)				
05)				

Step 4: Construct "I" statements defining the ultimate goal for each area (i.e. I am 220lb at 12% bodyfat and inspire others to be their best self while making a living off fitness).

❖ Consider conflicts with the life we live now that needs to go?

RECOMMENDED READINGS

Health

1) Carnegie, Dale. How to Stop Worrying and Start Living.

2) Goleman, Daniel. Vital Lies, Simple Truths: The Psychology of Self-Deception.

3) Greene, Robert-. The Daily Laws: 366 Meditations on Power, Seduction, Mastery, Strategy, and Human Nature.

4) Romaniello, John, and Adam Bornstein. Man 2.0 Engineering the Alpha.

Growth

5) Abrams, Jeremiah, and Connie Zweig. Meeting the Shadow : The Hidden Power of the Dark Side of Human Nature.

6) Aurelius, Marcus. Meditations.

7) Campbell, Joseph. The Hero with a Thousand Faces : A Brilliant Examination, through Ancient Hero

Myths, of Man's Eternal Struggle for Identity.

8) Clear, James. Atomic Habits.

9) Csikszentmihalyi, Mihaly. Flow: The Psychology of Optimal Experience.

10) Doidge, Norman. The Brain That Changes Itself: Stories of Personal Triumph from the Frontiers of Brain Science.

11) Dutton, Kevin. The Wisdom of Psychopaths.

12) Frederich Nietzsche. Thus Spake Zarathustra.

13) Greene, Robert. Mastery.

14) Hartmann, Franz. Magic, White and Black.

15) Hill, Napoleon, et al. Outwitting the Devil : The Secret to Freedom and Success.

16) Laozi, and D C Lau. Tao Te Ching.

17) Olson, Jeff, and John David Mann. The Slight Edge.

18) Peterson, Jordan B. 12 Rules for Life: An Antidote to Chaos.

19) Talbot, Michael. The Holographic Universe.

Wealth

20) 50 Cent, and Robert Greene. The 50th Law

21) Allen, David. Getting Things Done: The Art of Stress-Free Productivity

22) Cardone, Grant. Sell or Be Sold : How to Get Your Way in Business and in Life.

23) Cardone, Grant. The 10X Rule : The Only Difference between Success and Failure.

24) Ferriss, Timothy. The 4-Hour Workweek : Escape 9-5, Live Anywhere, and Join the New Rich.

25) Gerber, Michael E. The E-Myth.

26) Greene, Robert. The 33 Strategies of War.

27) Greene, Robert. The 48 Laws of Power.

28) Hill, Napoleon. The Law of Success.

29) Hill, Napoleon. Think & Grow Rich.

30) Kiyosaki, Robert T. Rich Dad Poor Dad.

31) Machiavelli, Niccolò. The Prince.

32) Samit, Jay. Disrupt You! : Master Personal Transformation, Seize Opportunity, and Thrive in the Era of Endless Innovation.

33) Samit, Jay. Future Proofing You : Twelve Truths for Creating Opportunity, Maximizing Wealth, and Controlling Your Destiny in an Uncertain World.

34) Stanley, Thomas J. The Millionaire next Door.

35) Tzu, Sun. The Art of War.

Relationships

36) Carnegie, Dale. How to Win Friends and Influence People.

37) Deida, David. Way of the Superior Man : A Spiritual Guide to Mastering the Challenges of Women, Work, and Sexual Desire. Sounds True, Incorporated, 2017.

38) Goleman, Daniel. Social Intelligence: The New Science of Human Relationships.

39) Greene, Robert. The Art of Seduction.

ABOUT THE AUTHOR

A Bridge Between Logic and Fulfillment, The Author of Integrate: ANGEL LOPEZ brings a unique blend of engineering, sales, and personal development expertise to help individuals cultivate strong relationships and achieve their goals. With a decade in the personal development field, four years as a relationship coach and acquiring various NLP certifications; writing the manual to an integrated life was the next logical decision.

*My journey to becoming the author of "**Integrate: The Secret To Harmony and The Pursuit of Purpose**" might seem unconventional. I began my career rooted in the logic and precision of mechanical engineering. However, this background became the launchpad for a profound shift towards understanding the human experience and a decade-long deep dive in the world of personal development. My transition to a top-performing sales engineer honed my communication and relationship-building skills to connect with people on a deeper level. This desire to foster connection extended beyond the sales floor. From the Engineer mind; I bring a methodical approach to problem-solving with clear, step-by-step framework for integrating the four pillars of life. Just as I once tackled complex engineering challenges, I wanted to systematically create a life of harmony. The Salesperson in me adds persuasiveness, the art of influencing and motivating others to help you get what you want. The Coach in me brings you honed an ability to truly understand human struggles and aspirations by offering practical guidance. I hope you enjoy.*

Learn more at: **www.IntegrateBook.com**.